D1519126

Old Southern COOKERY

Mary Randolph's
Recipes from
America's First Regional Cookbook
Adapted for Today's Kitchen

SUE J. HENDRICKS AND
CHRISTOPHER E. HENDRICKS

Historic Savannah Foundation

Globe
Pequot
Guilford, Connecticut

Globe Pequot

An imprint of The Rowman & Littlefield Publishing Group, Inc.
4501 Forbes Blvd., Ste. 200
Lanham, MD 2706
www.rowman.com

Distributed by NATIONAL BOOK NETWORK

Food photography by Deborah Llewellyn: pages iii, xvi, 18, 30, 46, 70, 106, 128, 136, 142, 144, 166, 168, 174, 194, 196, 226, and 234

Additional food photography by Jason B. James: pages 40, 48, 78, 110, 148, and 222

British Library Cataloguing in Publication Information available

Library of Congress Cataloging-in-Publication Data available

ISBN 978-1-4930-4905-9 (cloth: alk. paper)
ISBN 978-1-4930-4906-6 (electronic)

♾™ The paper used in this publication meets the minimum requirements of American National Standard for Information Sciences—Permanence of Paper for Printed Library Materials, ANSI/NISO Z39.48-1992

In memory of J. Edwin Hendricks,
loving husband and father,
who inspired this project with a gift

CONTENTS

FOREWORDS

Women have been at the core of Historic Savannah Foundation since its establishment in 1955. When seven visionary women saw the Isaiah Davenport House (1820) as more than a blighted, aging, hulk—that it was worthy of preservation—thus began an organization that fostered a movement which, in turn, sparked a renaissance that Savannah has enjoyed for more than a half century. Mary Randolph was a visionary in her own right. Her recipes and, more importantly, her cooking system recognized, taught, and celebrated regional fare. . . particularly Southern cooking. As a lagniappe, she included insights into Southern traditions and the role of women.

Like Historic Savannah Foundation's founders who gazed upon the Davenport House, Mary Randolph saw more than what was there. They understood that one old building (or one old recipe) may not change the world, but a collection of them can. Indeed, it has. Mary Randolph's pioneering and widely published cookbook has educated numerous and deliciously fed generations. Likewise, Historic Savannah Foundation has saved more than four hundred buildings and inspired other cities and organizations to use a revolving fund to acquire and save endangered historic buildings.

The foundation and the Isaiah Davenport House, now its flagship property, are grateful to the authors for reviving a historic record of cooking in the South, but also for updating it and making it relevant today. When the Historic Savannah Foundation saves historic buildings, the real success comes when that building is rehabilitated for contemporary use. The recipes for these successes are tried and true. Whether it's turtle soup or turnip ragout . . . or whether it's a turreted Queen Ann or a modest shotgun . . . Mary Randolph (and now Sue Hendricks and Chris Hendricks) and Historic Savannah Foundation are serving up history in the twenty-first century.

The icing on the (Savoy Sponge) cake is that proceeds from the sale of this book directly support the mission of Historic Savannah Foundation and the stewardship of the Davenport House. The foundation saves buildings, places, and stories that define Savannah's past, present, and future. This cookbook is helping us do just that.

The foresight of the Hendricks family to preserve and promote Southern culinary heritage and one of the South's most beautiful cities cannot be overstated. We are grateful for their wisdom and generosity.

Daniel G. Carey

Past President and CEO (2008-2019)
Historic Savannah Foundation

In conjuring up a list of earthly delights, Southern cooking ranks high for many. The anthropologist in us wonders how these miracles of gastronomy came to be: okra soup, fried perch, macaroni and cheese, and sweet potato pie!

The first person to codify and publish recipes in the American Southeast was Mary Randolph of Virginia. Her work is the genesis for documenting regional cooking that has become world renowned. People, like myself, who work in historic sites and house museums and whose job it is to tell the story of daily life in the Antebellum South, have for years looked to a facsimile of Randolph's 1824 cookbook for source material. When Chris Hendricks, a friend and a well-respected (and beloved) scholar of eighteenth and nineteenth century history, told me that he and his mother, Sue Hendricks, a former journalist, were updating Randolph's *The Virginia Housewife* for contemporary cooks, I was delighted. I thought to myself, *Every historic house curator and foodie interested in heritage cooking in the Southeast is going to want a copy.*

While Randolph's work provides fantastic documentation of historic recipes, recreating her recipes is tricky, and for many, like myself, a mystery of the past. For example, interpreting the meaning of "shake oysters over the fire till they are quite hot . . ." in making oyster sauce for a turkey proved an insurmountable obstacle.

Several years ago, a colleague studying visitor motivation at Colonial Williamsburg said that visitors often say the reason they wanted to come to the restored town was to be transported back in time. They wanted to be "back then" or at least be awash in authenticity. You cannot get the same sense of "back then" by reading a recipe, as you can by eating the food in question. You have to taste it! How exciting it is to have treasured heritage recipes translated into a version that can be created by the everyday cook. Thanks to Sue and Chris, we can now make reasonable versions, sans the open fire, of dishes that graced the tables of our forebears. For those of us in the house museum business, we can now provide our visitors, as well as our friends and family, with a richer and tastier understanding of the past that reverberates today. All of this talk makes me want an apple fritter (see page 194)!

Jamie Credle

Director
Davenport House Museum, a property of Historic Savannah Foundation

ACKNOWLEDGMENTS

The unusual nature of this endeavor required the assistance of many talented individuals with diverse skills. The research for the book took place at several academic institutions, but we particularly would like to thank the staffs of the John D. Rockefeller Jr. Library at the Colonial Williamsburg Foundation, the Martha Blakeney Hodges Special Collections and University Archives at the University of North Carolina at Greensboro, Chris Semtner of the Edgar Allan Poe Museum in Richmond, and especially Pam Seay of the Virginia Historical Society for her patronage of the project and for overseeing the peer review process. With her boundless energy and enthusiasm, Jamie Credle, director of the Davenport House Museum, lent constant and unflagging support, even offering the use of the museum's porcelain collection for the photography. Daniel Carey and Susan Adler of the museum's parent institution, the Historic Savannah Foundation, backed the effort and worked to ensure its quality and academic character. We thank Janice Shay for sharing her experience and guidance as we worked through the design and publication process; Deborah Llewellyn and Jason James for their excellent photography; Erin Purdy for her remarkable transcription work; Greta and Quinn Bledsoe for making a special trip over to Arlington; Cindi Pietryzk for her skillful copy editing; and Ma Ni for her help during the photo shoots. Jennifer McCarthy lent invaluable assistance in too many ways to even begin to recount. Thanks to Katherine Durso and David Riemen for their help in food production. Thank you to the members of our family—Jim and Lisa, Lee and Dennis, Grayson, and William—for their love and support. And finally, thank you to Brian Martine, who acted as sous-chef, art director, and chief supporter. This book could not have happened without any of you.

INTRODUCTION

When Mary Randolph (1762–1828) published her cookbook, *The Virginia House-Wife,* almost two centuries ago, she created an American classic. Although initially she had difficulty finding a publisher for the work, after it first appeared in 1824, it became a bestseller. Randolph was working on the third edition when she died just four years later. A Baltimore firm picked up the book and published it again in 1831 and1838. Its acclaim grew well beyond a regional audience and spread into the North. A Philadelphia publisher released the work in 1850. In all it went through nineteen editions before the outbreak of the Civil War, and the book has mostly been in print for 190 years. There are several reasons for its longevity. It was the first regional American cookbook; the first published work on Southern cooking. Some food scholars credit it with being the first authentically American cookbook, period. The book is a fascinating historical document, providing insight into Southern culture, food traditions, household organization and management, and women's position and role in society.[1] However, *The Virginia Housewife* (the hyphen in the title disappeared with publication of the fourth edition in 1840)[2] has survived for another reason: Good recipes never fade; Randolph's food is delicious.

This collection of Mary Randolph's recipes began as a gift. My father, a history professor at Wake Forest University, picked up a copy of the 1860 edition of *The Virginia Housewife* while on a research trip as a present for my mother, a cookbook collector. Fascinated, she worked her way through the recipes over the next year, converting them into versions she could use at home. Originally, she just meant the recipes for personal use, but over time, more and more people began asking for copies of the updated recipes. These were not just friends. Interpreters at different historic sites began to express interest as well, because Mary Randolph's work is the go-to source for museums of the colonial and antebellum periods for interpreting foodways and domestic culture.

A couple of years ago, while I was helping my parents move into a new home, I ran across my mother's interpretations of Randolph's recipes.

Intrigued, I spent time at various repositories in Virginia investigating the history of Mary Randolph and *The Virginia Housewife*. After returning to Savannah, I attended a reception at the Davenport House Museum and while talking with Jamie Credle, the director, I asked her if the museum used Randolph's book. Credle grew animated and told me about workshops and cooking symposia she had attended that used Randolph's book as their centerpiece. She declared, "It's the touchstone for anything we do; interpreting the food at teas, our Christmas celebrations, anything. It's the ready reference that anyone interpreting the early nineteenth century needs to have on their bookshelf. We're using it to help with the reinterpretation of our kitchen space right now." A number of conversations followed and this book is the result.

What follows is a collection of Mary Randolph's recipes along with the story of Mary Randolph and her contributions to American culinary history. Each recipe has the original text from *The Virginia Housewife* followed by a contemporary version noting modern temperatures, measurements, substitute ingredients, etc. We have not included every recipe. To Make Jelly from Feet and To Prepare Cosmetic Soap for Washing the Hands are not included, for example. And while the order of the recipes mostly follows the order in which they appeared in the original, we have done some rearranging. While Randolph mostly grouped her recipes by type—meats, vegetables, etc.—occasionally she seems to have arranged foods together by association. For example, although she included To Make a Dish of Curry after the East Indian Manner with other chicken dishes, she immediately followed it with Dish of Rice to be Served up with the Curry, in a Dish by Itself, followed by two okra recipes she may very well have served alongside the curry. It is our hope that this book and our organization of recipes will help make Randolph's work more accessible to cooks of all stripes as they enjoy the art of Southern cookery.

Christopher E. Hendricks

Georgia Southern University
Savannah, Georgia

Asparagus Chicken Soup

Chapter 1

SOUPS

ASPARAGUS SOUP.

TAKE four large bunches of asparagus, scrape it nicely, cut off one inch of the tops, and lay them in water, chop the stalks and put them on the fire with a piece of bacon, a large onion cut up, and pepper and salt; add two quarts of water, boil them till the stalks are quite soft, then pulp them through a sieve, and strain the water to it, which must be put back in the pot; put into it a chicken cut up, with the tops of asparagus which had been laid by, boil it until these last articles are sufficiently done, thicken with flour, butter and milk, and serve it up.

Asparagus Chicken Soup

SERVES 4

A well-stocked nineteenth-century kitchen would have had a variety of sieves and strainers of different gauges for purposes such as removing chaff from grain, sifting flour, or separating solid and liquid objects. Sieves would have been made with a wooden or metal mesh, or simply by punching holes into sheet metal. For pressing vegetables into a pulp, a wide mesh is best, or if one is not available, a boiling basket or metal colander. Or it is possible to puree the vegetables in a food processor or blender.

1 large bunch asparagus

¼ pound bacon

1 medium onion, chopped

Salt and pepper, to taste

1 cup cubed (approximately 5 ounces), cooked chicken

1 cup white sauce (recipe below)

For the White Sauce:

2 tablespoons flour

2 tablespoons butter, melted

1 cup milk

Wash the asparagus and cut 1 inch off the tops, saving the tops in a bowl of cool water.

Cut the asparagus stalks into 1-inch pieces and place them in a medium saucepan with the bacon, onion, salt, and pepper. Add enough water to cover, and bring to a simmer over medium-high heat, then reduce the heat to medium and continue to simmer 10 to 12 minutes, or until the asparagus is very soft.

Remove the asparagus from the saucepan and press through a fine mesh sieve into the stock.

Strain the remaining stock, discard the bacon pieces and onion, and return the broth to the saucepan.

Add the chicken and asparagus tops to the saucepan and bring to a boil over medium-high heat, then reduce the heat to medium-low and simmer 10 minutes.

To make the White Sauce

In a small saucepan, whisk together the flour and butter; add the milk a little at a time, whisking to incorporate. Bring to boil over medium-high heat, stirring constantly, until the sauce has thickened. You may add more milk for a thinner sauce.

Add the white sauce to the chicken and asparagus soup; blend well, and return to low heat until warmed through. Serve hot.

BEEF SOUP.

TAKE the hind shin of beef, cut off all the flesh off the leg-bone, which must be taken away entirely, or the soup will be greasy. Wash the meat clean and lay it in a pot, sprinkle over it one small table-spoonful of pounded black pepper, and two of salt; three onions the size of a hen's egg, cut small, six small carrots scraped and cut up, two small turnips pared and cut into dice; pour on three quarts of water, cover the pot close, and keep it gently and steadily boiling five hours, which will leave about three pints of clear soup; do not let the pot boil over, but take off the scum carefully, as it rises. When it has boiled four hours, put in a small bundle of thyme and parsley, and a pint of celery cut small, or a tea-spoonful of celery seed pounded. These latter ingredients would lose their delicate flavour if boiled too much. Just before you take it up, brown it in the following manner: put a small table-spoonful of nice brown sugar into an iron skillet, set it on the fire and stir it till it melts and looks very dark, pour into it a ladle full of the soup, a little at a time; stirring it all the while. Strain this browning and mix it well with the soup; take out the bundle of thyme and parsley, put the nicest pieces of meat in your tureen, and pour on the soup and vegetables; put in some toasted bread cut in dice, and serve it up.

Vegetable Beef Soup

SERVES 6-8

Browning sauces for gravies and meat dishes were well in use in Europe by the eighteenth century and often used brown sugar or molasses. Commercial browning sauces in the United States became available after the Civil War. Kitchen Bouquet, for example, went into production around 1873.

2 pounds lean beef, cut into 1-inch cubes

2 teaspoons salt

½ teaspoon pepper

1 small onion, thinly sliced

1 cup celery, diced

1 cup carrots, thinly sliced

1 cup turnips, diced

½ teaspoon thyme

1 tablespoon dried parsley flakes, or 2 tablespoons minced fresh parsley

1 tablespoon brown sugar (may substitute 2 teaspoons Kitchen Bouquet)

In a large lidded saucepan, add the beef, salt, pepper, and 4 to 6 cups of water. Bring to a boil over medium-high heat, then reduce the heat to low, cover, and simmer for 2 hours. Add the vegetables, herbs, and spices, and continue to simmer for 15 to 20 minutes, or until the vegetables are tender.

To brown the soup, melt the brown sugar in a separate small pan over low heat, stirring; do not let it burn. Stir the sugar into a small cup of the hot soup; then strain this and add it to the soup. Or add 2 teaspoons Kitchen Bouquet. Stir to combine. Serve hot.

SOUP WITH BOUILLI.

TAKE the nicest part of the thick brisket of beef, about eight pounds, put it into a pot with every thing directed for the other soup; make it exactly in the same way, only put it on an hour sooner, that you may have time to prepare the bouilli; after it has boiled five hours, take out the beef, cover up the soup and set it near the fire that it may keep hot. Take the skin off the beef, have the yelk of an egg well beaten, dip a feather in it and wash the top of your beef, sprinkle over it the crumb of stale bread finely grated, put it in a Dutch oven previously heated, put the top on with coals enough to brown, but not burn the beef; let it stand nearly an hour, and prepare your gravy thus:—Take a sufficient quantity of soup and the vegetables boiled in it; add to it a table-spoonful of red wine, and two of mushroom catsup, thicken with a little bit of butter and a little brown flour; make it very hot, pour it in your dish, and put the beef on it. Garnish it with green pickle, cut in thin slices, serve up the soup in a tureen with bits of toasted bread.

French Beef Stew

SERVES 6-8

Pot-au-Feu is a traditional family dish in France. Randolph may have learned the recipe during her family's summer trips to New England because the dish is known as Bouilli *in Quebec. First cut brisket is the lower half of the brisket and is the most common cut found in grocery stores. It sometimes is referred to as "flat."*

4 pounds beef (first cut brisket), whole

1 large onion, sliced

3 carrots, sliced

3 stalks celery, broken

1 turnip, quartered

2 tablespoons dried parsley flakes, or 4 tablespoons minced fresh parsley

3-4 whole peppercorns

1 tablespoon salt

1 egg yolk, beaten

2 cups bread crumbs

1 tablespoon red wine

2 tablespoons Mushroom Catsup (see page 156) or Worcestershire sauce

1 tablespoon flour

Place the beef in a heavy saucepan with the vegetables, parsley, and peppercorns. Cover with water and bring to a boil over medium-high heat. Continue to cook 5 minutes. Reduce the heat to low, skim off any froth, and add the salt. Cover and simmer for 2½ hours, or until the meat is tender.

Preheat oven to 325°F.

Use a slotted spoon to remove the cooked meat and transfer to parchment paper. Set the saucepan with the remaining vegetable broth aside to cool. Brush the beaten yolk over the whole brisket on all sides, then coat with the bread crumbs. Place the beef on a lightly greased sheet pan and bake 15 to 20 minutes, or until brown.

Meanwhile, stir the red wine and Mushroom Catsup (or Worcestershire sauce) into the vegetable broth.

Mix the flour with a little broth to make a paste and stir it into the remaining broth to thicken it.

Slice the brisket across the grain into 6 to 8 pieces and return it to the broth. Serve warm.

VEAL SOUP.

PUT into a pot three quarts of water, three onions cut small, one spoonful of black pepper pounded, and two of salt, with two or three slices of lean ham; let it boil steadily two hours; skim it occasionally, then put into it a shin of veal, let it boil two hours longer; take out the slices of ham, and skim off the grease if any should rise, take a gill of good cream, mix with it two table spoonsful of flour very nicely, and the yelks of two eggs beaten well, strain this mixture, and add some chopped parsley; pour some soup on by degrees, stir it well, and pour it into the pot, continuing to stir until it has boiled two or three minutes to take off the raw taste of the eggs. If the cream be not perfectly sweet, and the eggs quite new, the thickening will curdle in the soup. For a change you may put a dozen ripe tomatos in, first taking off their skins, by letting them stand a few minutes in hot water, when they may be easily peeled. When made in this way you must thicken it with the flour only. Any part of the veal may be used, but the shin or knuckle is the nicest.

Creamy Veal Soup

SERVES 8

Randolph would have dried herbs available for cooking year-round. Because dried herbs gain potency in flavor, she would have adjusted the amounts she used depending on how long they were stored.

3 medium onions, chopped

½ pound lean uncooked ham, cut into ¼-inch slices

2 teaspoons salt

1 teaspoon pepper

3 pounds veal, cut into ½-inch cubes

2 egg yolks, beaten

2 tablespoons flour

½ cup heavy cream or 10–12 small (or 32-ounce can) tomatoes, peeled

2 tablespoons dried parsley flakes or 4 tablespoons minced fresh parsley

Place the onions, ham, salt, and pepper in a heavy pan along with 2 quarts water, bring just to a boil over medium-high heat, then reduce the heat to low, and simmer 2 hours, stirring and skimming off the froth occasionally.

Add the veal cubes, and additional water as needed to keep ingredients covered. Continue to simmer for another 2 hours. Remove the ham and discard. Skim off any remaining grease in the pan.

In a separate bowl, beat the egg yolks, and whisk in the flour and cream. Add the parsley. Slowly stir this into the soup, and cook on low heat for 5 to 7 minutes, stirring occasionally. Serve hot.

For variety, use tomatoes instead of the cream mixture. In a separate bowl, beat the egg yolks, and whisk in the flour and ½ cup of the broth. Add tomatoes and parsley. Slowly stir this into the soup, and cook on low heat for 5 to 7 minutes, stirring occasionally.

OYSTER SOUP.

WASH and drain two quarts of oysters, put them on with three quarts of water, three onions chopped up, two or three slices of lean ham, pepper and salt; boil it till reduced one-half, strain it through a sieve, return the liquid into the pot, put in one quart of fresh oysters, boil it till they are sufficiently done, and thicken the soup with four spoonsful of flour, two gills of rich cream, and the yelks of six new laid eggs beaten well; boil it a few minutes after the thickening is put in. Take care that it does not curdle, and that the flour is not in lumps; serve it up with the last oysters that were put in. If the flavour of thyme be agreeable, you may put in a little, but take care that it does not boil in it long enough to discolour the soup.

Oyster Stew

SERVES 4

Native Americans along the Atlantic coast harvested oysters for thousands of years before European contact. The discarded shells created mounds, or middens, that were often several yards high. During the difficult years of early settlement when food was short, British settlers in Virginia emulated native groups and ate oysters for survival, but later began harvesting them for sale to inland towns and the Caribbean.

2 pints oysters, washed

1 medium onion, chopped

1 small slice lean uncooked ham

Salt and pepper, to taste

⅓ cup cream

1½ tablespoons flour

2 egg yolks, beaten

¼ teaspoon thyme (optional)

Combine 1 pint oysters, the onions, ham, salt, pepper, and 1 quart water in a medium saucepan. Bring to a boil over medium-high heat and continue to boil until the broth has reduced by half. Strain and return the liquid to the pan; discard the ham and oysters. Add the second pint of oysters to the pan over medium heat and simmer 2 minutes, or until they begin to curl.

In a small bowl, whisk the flour into the cream, stir in the egg yolks, and add the mixture to the soup. Return the pot to medium-high and boil 2 to 3 minutes. Season to taste and serve hot.

BARLEY SOUP.

PUT on three gills of barley, three quarts of water, few onions cut up, six carrots scraped and cut into dice, an equal quantity of turnips cut small; boil it gently two hours, then put in four or five pounds of the rack or neck of mutton, a few slices of lean ham, with pepper and salt; boil it slowly two hours longer and serve it up. Tomatos are an excellent addition to this soup.

Lamb and Barley Soup

SERVES 8-10

Lamb and Barley Soup, or Scotch Broth, is a hearty soup that dates back at least to the seventeenth century. You may substitute hulled barley, which retains its bran and has a higher nutrient content, although both pearl and hulled barley are high in fiber.

½ cup pearl barley

3 pounds lamb

½ pound lean uncooked ham, cut into ½-inch cubes

2 medium onions, thinly sliced

1 cup carrots, diced

1 cup turnips, diced

4 tomatoes, quartered

Salt and pepper, to taste

Soak the barley in a pot with 2 cups water for 12 hours, then drain and rinse.

In a stockpot over medium heat, add the barley, lamb, and ham with enough water to cover. Simmer covered for 2 hours.

Add the vegetables, salt, and pepper, and water as needed to keep ingredients covered. Continue to simmer for 30 minutes, or until the vegetables are tender. Remove the meat, dice it, and return it to the soup. Stir in a little flour if the soup needs to be thicker. Serve warm.

DRIED PEA SOUP.

TAKE one quart of split peas, or Lima beans, which are better; put them in three quarts of very soft water with three onions chopped up, pepper and salt; boil them two hours; mash them well and pass them through a sieve; return the liquid into the pot, thicken it with a large piece of butter and flour, put in some slices of nice salt pork, and a large tea-spoonful of celery seed pounded; boil it till the pork is done, and serve it up; have some toasted bread cut into dice and fried in butter, which must be put in the tureen before you pour in the soup.

Split Pea Soup with Croutons

SERVES 12

Lima beans originated in Central and South America. The Spanish encountered them in the sixteenth century after conquering the Incan Empire and named the beans after Lima, Peru. Lima beans are a quintessential Southern food, and are often stored dried, which made it easy for Randolph to use them as a substitute for split peas.

For the soup:

1 quart split peas or lima beans

3 medium onions, chopped

Salt and pepper, to taste

¼ pound salt pork

1 teaspoon celery seed, or ½ cup fresh celery, diced

2 tablespoons butter

2 tablespoons flour

For the Croutons:

Small loaf stale bread, crusts removed

½ cup butter

To make the soup

Put peas and 3 quarts water in a large saucepan over medium-high heat with the onions, salt, and pepper. Bring to a boil, cover, reduce heat, and simmer for 2 hours.

Press the soup through a sieve. Return the liquid to the pot over medium-high heat, add the pork and celery seed. Boil 10 minutes, or until the pork is cooked through, then reduce the heat to simmer.

In a separate pan, melt the butter and stir in flour. Add to soup to thicken. Serve with croutons.

To make the Croutons

Cube the bread into desired size.

Melt the butter in a frying pan over medium-high heat and add the bread cubes. Fry, turning, until light brown on all sides.

GREEN PEA SOUP.

MAKE it exactly as you do the dried pea soup, only in place of the celery seed, put a handful of mint chopped small, and a pint of young peas, which must be boiled in the soup till tender; thicken it with a quarter of a pound of butter, and two spoonsful of flour.

Fresh Pea and Mint Soup with Croutons

SERVES 6

Fresh Pea and Mint Soup, or Potage Saint-Germain, is a French dish that developed in the area of Saint-Germain-en-Laye, a suburb of Paris. This soup is made the same as the Split Pea Soup, substituting young shelled peas for the split peas, and using chopped mint in the place of the celery.

For the Soup:

- 1 pint young shelled peas (or 10 ounces frozen peas, thawed and rinsed)
- 3 medium onions, chopped
- Salt and pepper, to taste
- ¼ pound salt pork
- 1 cup chopped mint
- 2 tablespoons butter
- 2 tablespoons flour

For the Croutons:

- Small loaf stale bread, crusts removed
- ½ cup butter

To make the soup

Put peas and 3 quarts water in a large saucepan over medium-high heat with the onions, salt, and pepper. Bring to a boil, cover, and continue to boil for 3 to 5 minutes.

Press the soup through a sieve. Return the liquid to the pot over medium-high heat, add the pork and mint. Boil 10 minutes, or until the pork is cooked through, then reduce the heat to simmer.

In a separate pan, melt the butter and stir in flour. Add to soup to thicken. Serve over or garnish with croutons.

To make the Croutons

Cube the bread into desired size.

Melt the butter in a frying pan over medium-high heat and add the bread cubes. Fry, turning, until light brown on all sides.

Ochra Soup.

GET two double handsful of young ochra, wash and slice it thin, add two onions chopped fine, put it into a gallon of water at a very early hour in an earthen pipkin, or very nice iron pot; it must be kept steadily simmering, but not boiling: put in pepper and salt. At 12 o'clock, put in a handful of Lima beans; at half-past one o'clock, add three young cimlins cleaned and cut in small pieces, a fowl, or knuckle of veal, a bit of bacon or pork that has been boiled, and six tomatos, with the skin taken off; when nearly done, thicken with a spoonful of butter, mixed with one of flour. Have rice boiled to eat with it.

Virginia Gumbo

SERVES 8-10

Virginia Gumbo or okra soup is a good example of how African foodways influenced Southern cooking. Okra is a staple in West African cooking and was brought to North America along with enslaved people. It was introduced in the Southern British colonies early in the eighteenth century.

1 teaspoon salt

2 cups okra, thinly sliced

2 medium onions, diced

1 cup lima beans

3 small yellow squashes, cut into ½-inch cubes

6 tomatoes, peeled and quartered, or 2 cups canned tomatoes

1½ pounds chicken or veal, cut into 1-inch cubes

Salt and pepper, to taste

2 tablespoons butter, melted

2 tablespoons flour

¼ pound bacon, cooked, drained, and broken into small pieces

In a medium saucepan on medium-high heat, bring 2 quarts water and 1 teaspoon salt to a boil, add the okra, and continue to boil for 10 minutes. Add the remaining vegetables and the chicken or veal. Reduce the heat to medium-low and simmer for 10 to 15 minutes, or until the vegetables are tender and the meat is cooked.

In a small bowl, make a paste of the butter and flour and stir it into the soup to thicken. Add the bacon crumbles and serve in bowls. May be served over rice. Salt and pepper, to taste

HARE OR RABBIT SOUP.

CUT up two hares, put them into a pot with a piece of bacon, two onions chopped, a bundle of thyme and parsley, which must be taken out before the soup is thickened, add pepper, salt, pounded cloves, and mace, put in a sufficient quantity of water, stew it gently three hours, thicken with a large spoonful of butter, and one of brown flour, with a glass of red wine; boil it a few minutes longer, and serve it up with the nicest parts of the hares. Squirrels make soup equally good, done the same way.

Rabbit Stew

SERVES 4

Rabbit stew is a dish common in many cultures across Europe and is also a traditional dish among Native American peoples, including the Algonquins. Rabbits were plentiful in North America and were both hunted and raised domestically. Rabbit meat today can be found in a surprising number of grocery store chains, local butchers, or through Internet outlets.

1 rabbit, cleaned and cut into serving pieces

1 cup flour

Salt and pepper, to taste

¼ pound bacon

4 tablespoons butter

2 medium onions, thinly sliced

½ teaspoon thyme

1 tablespoon dried parsley flakes, or 2 tablespoons minced fresh parsley

1 teaspoon ground cloves

½ teaspoon mace

1 cup red wine

Wash and clean the rabbit pieces in warm water and pat dry with paper towels.

Put the flour in a shallow bowl and dredge the rabbit pieces to coat overall. Sprinkle the pieces with salt and pepper.

Cook the bacon in a large skillet over medium high heat, and remove to drain on paper towels.

Heat the butter in the bacon grease (or substitute olive oil) over medium-high heat. Fry the rabbit pieces for 2 to 3 minutes on each side until golden brown.

Crumble and add the bacon along with the onions, spices, and enough water to cover, reduce the heat to medium-low and simmer for 1 hour, adding water if necessary.

Stir in the wine and bring just to a boil, then remove from heat and serve immediately.

SOUP OF ANY KIND OF OLD FOWL.

The only way in which they are eatable.

PUT the fowls in a coop and feed them moderately for a fortnight; kill one and cleanse it, cut off the legs and wings, and separate the breast from the ribs, which, together with the whole back, must be thrown away, being too gross and strong for use. Take the skin and fat from the parts cut off which are also gross. Wash the pieces nicely, and put them on the fire with about a pound of bacon, a large onion chopped small, some pepper and salt, a few blades of mace, a handful of parsley, cut up very fine, and two quarts of water, if it be a common fowl or duck—a turkey will require more water. Boil it gently for three hours, tie up a small bunch of thyme, and let it boil in it half an hour, then take it out. Thicken your soup with a large spoonful of butter rubbed into two of flour, the yelks of two eggs, and half a pint of milk. Be careful not to let it curdle in the soup.

Creamy Chicken Soup

SERVES 10-12

Randolph never let food go to waste and her recipe for Soup of Any Kind of Old Fowl is a good example of this. A hen can lay eggs for five or more years. After its productive life is over, the chicken can be cooked, but the meat is tough and has to be prepared carefully. Randolph created her recipe with that in mind.

1 (3- to 5-pound) fowl (whole chicken, turkey breast, game hens, etc.), skin on, and cut into pieces

¼ pound bacon, cooked and crumbled

1 large onion, sliced

¼ teaspoon mace

¼ cup dried parsley flakes or ½ cup minced fresh parsley

Salt and pepper, to taste

¼ teaspoon thyme

1 tablespoon flour

2 tablespoons butter

2 egg yolks

1 cup milk

Wash the fowl and trim away any excess fat. Place the pieces in a large pan with the bacon crumbles, onion, herbs, and spices, and enough water to cover. Bring to boil over medium-high heat, then reduce the heat to medium-low and simmer for 1½ to 2 hours, skimming froth from the surface occasionally, until the meat is tender and falling off the bone. Add enough water as necessary to keep the meat covered during cooking.

Remove the fowl from the pan, remove and discard the bones, and cut the meat in small pieces. Return the meat to the soup.

To thicken, make a paste of butter, flour, egg yolks, and a little of the hot stock in a small bowl. Stir the milk into the paste, then stir the paste into the soup. Serve hot.

CATFISH SOUP.

An excellent dish for those who have not imbibed a needless prejudice against those delicious fish.

TAKE two large or four small white catfish that have been caught in deep water, cut off the heads, and skin and clean the bodies; cut each in three parts, put them in a pot, with a pound of lean bacon, a large onion cut up, a handful of parsley chopped small, some pepper and salt, pour in a sufficient quantity of water, and stew them till the fish are quite tender but not broken; beat the yelks of four fresh eggs, add to them a large spoonful of butter, two of flour, and half a pint of rich milk; make all these warm and thicken the soup, take out the bacon, and put some of the fish in your tureen, pour in the soup, and serve it up.

Creamy Catfish Soup

SERVES 6

This recipe is for bisque, a creamy soup that developed in France. Based on her comment underneath the recipe title, customers at Randolph's boarding house may have felt catfish had a poor reputation, although it was served commonly in the Southeast during the colonial and early national periods.

4 small white catfish, cleaned, deboned, and cut into pieces

1 pound bacon, cut into 1-inch pieces

1 large onion, coarsely chopped

½ cup dried parsley flakes, or 1 cup minced fresh parsley

2 tablespoons flour

1 tablespoon butter

1 cup cream

Salt and pepper, to taste

Place the fish, bacon, onion, and parsley into a stockpot with 2 quarts water. Bring to a gentle boil over medium-high heat and cook 30 minutes, or until the fish flakes easily and the onions are tender. Lower the heat to medium-low. Remove the bacon and discard.

In a small bowl, combine the flour, butter, and cream. Stir until smooth, then add this to the soup, stirring to integrate. Continue to simmer, stirring frequently, until the soup thickens. Serve hot.

ONION SOUP.

CHOP up twelve large onions, boil them in three quarts of milk and water equally mixed, put in a bit of veal or fowl, and a piece of bacon with pepper and salt. When the onions are boiled to pulp, thicken it with a large spoonful of butter mixed with one of flour. Take out the meat, and serve it up with toasted bread cut in small pieces in the soup.

Creamy French Onion Soup

SERVES 12

French onion soup normally features onions that have been caramelized, i.e. sautéed in sugar. This style of onion soup is favored in the French province of Normandy.

12 large onions, diced

½ pound bacon

6 cups chicken stock

6 cups whole milk

Salt and pepper, to taste

2 tablespoons flour

1 tablespoon butter, melted, plus more to butter toast

1 small baguette

Place the onions, bacon, and chicken stock in a large stockpot, bring to a boil over medium-high heat. Boil, stirring occasionally, until the onions are pulpy.

Lower the heat to medium-low and add the milk, salt, and pepper, and simmer for 30 minutes. Remove the bacon and discard.

In a small bowl, blend the flour with 1 tablespoon butter and a little soup to make a smooth paste. Stir this into the soup to thicken.

Slice the baguette on the diagonal. Butter and toast the slices, then cover the soup. Serve either in a tureen or in individual bowls.

MOCK TURTLE SOUP OF CALF'S HEAD.

HAVE a large head cleaned nicely without taking off the skin, divide the chop from the front of the head, take out the tongue, (which is best when salted,) put on the head with a gallon of water, the hock of a ham or a piece of nice pork, four or five onions, thyme, parsley, cloves and nutmeg, pepper and salt, boil all these together until the flesh on the head is quite tender, then take it up, cut all into small pieces, take the eyes out carefully, strain the water in which it was boiled, add half a pint of wine and a gill of mushroom catsup, let it boil slowly till reduced to two quarts, thicken it with two spoonsful of browned flour rubbed into four ounces of butter, put the meat in, and after stewing it a short time, serve it up. The eyes are a great delicacy.

Mock Turtle Soup

SERVES 6-8

Colonial settlers began making turtle soup using green snapping turtles early in the seventeenth century. It became wildly popular, so much so that Randolph included detailed instructions on how to "dress" a turtle in her cookbook. People ate so many turtles and tortoises during the Great Depression that their populations declined, and the soup fell out of favor.

Mock turtle soup recipes developed as a way to use organ meats, which simulated the texture of turtle meat; however, other meats make excellent substitutes.

1 pound ground sirloin

½ cup butter

2 cups cooked and cubed ham

¼ teaspoon thyme

2 tablespoons dried parsley flakes, or 4 tablespoons minced fresh parsley

½ teaspoon nutmeg

½ teaspoon cloves

1 onion, diced

2 tablespoons flour

1 tablespoon butter, melted

2 cups chicken broth

2 cups beef broth

1 cup white wine

½ cup Mushroom Catsup (see page 156), or Worcestershire sauce

Salt and pepper, to taste

Brown the beef quickly in a large skillet over medium-high heat, and drain the fat. Set aside.

Melt the butter in a separate large saucepan over medium heat. Add the ham, thyme, parsley, nutmeg, cloves, and onion and sauté 3 to 5 minutes until the onion is translucent.

In a small bowl, make a smooth paste using the flour and butter; stir this into the saucepan with the ham and onions. Add the cooked beef, chicken broth, beef broth, wine, Mushroom Catsup, salt, and pepper and stir. Increase the heat to high and bring to a quick boil, then reduce the heat to low and simmer until the soup thickens. Serve hot.

CHOWDER, A SEA DISH.

TAKE any kind of firm fish, cut it in pieces six inches long, sprinkle salt and pepper over each piece, cover the bottom of a small Dutch oven with slices of salt pork about half boiled, lay in the fish, strewing a little chopped onion between; cover with crackers that have been soaked soft in milk, pour over it two gills of white wine, and two of water; put on the top of the oven, and stew it gently about an hour; take it out carefully, and lay it in a deep dish; thicken the gravy with a little flour and a spoonful of butter, add some chopped parsley, boil it a few minutes, and pour it over the fish—serve it up hot.

Fish Chowder

SERVES 4

Chowder is a dish that originated onboard ships during long voyages. The name may be derived from the French word chaudron, *or cauldron. Breton fishermen brought the dish to French Canada and it spread throughout the American colonies.*

3 tablespoons butter, divided

1 pound any firm white fish (cod, pollock, halibut, striped bass, etc.)

Salt and pepper, to taste

1 onion, minced

4 strips bacon, cut up

1½ cups crumbled saltine crackers

1 cup whole milk

1 cup white wine

1 tablespoon flour

1 tablespoon parsley

Coat the bottom of a Dutch oven with 1 tablespoon butter.

Cut the fish into 6-inch pieces, sprinkle with salt and pepper, and arrange in the Dutch oven. Sprinkle the onion and bacon over the fish.

Soak the crackers in the milk and pour over the fish along with 1 cup water and the wine. Cover and simmer for 1 hour, adding water if necessary to cover ingredients. Remove the fish to a serving dish.

Melt the remaining butter in a cup and mix in the flour and parsley to make a paste. Add this to the soup and stir to thicken. Return fish to soup and serve.

THE STORY OF
Mary Randolph

Mary Randolph was a member of one of the oldest and most distinguished families in Virginia. Tracing their roots to Pocahontas and John Rolfe during the earliest years of the colony's establishment, the Randolph family flourished, growing into several branches. Mary's father, Thomas Mann Randolph (1741–1794), was orphaned at the age of five and became the ward of surveyor and mapmaker Peter Jefferson. Jefferson moved his wife, Jane Randolph Jefferson, and their son Thomas to Tuckahoe, a Randolph plantation on the north bank of the James River west of Richmond. There the two Thomases were raised like brothers. Thomas Randolph married Anne Cary (1745–1789) and the couple had thirteen children. Mary, known as Molly in the family, was their oldest. She and her siblings were educated by private tutors in reading, writing, and mathematics. And as a member of one of Virginia's elite families, Molly also learned and mastered the domestic skills necessary to run a large estate.[1] She put all those skills to use when, in 1780 at the age of eighteen, she married her cousin David Meade Randolph (1760–1830). The young couple settled at Presqu'île in Chesterfield County, part of the extensive Randolph family holdings along the James, which David received from his father upon his marriage.[2]

Through effort and scientific farming, David made Presqu'île into a financial success, earning a reputation as an excellent planter. When he visited the Randolphs in 1796, French social reformer the Duc de la Rochefoucauld-Liancourt declared that David was "fully entitled to the reputation which he enjoys of being the best farmer in the whole country."[3] But David also had political ambitions. The Randolph family had a long and storied career in Virginia politics and David asked his cousin, Secretary of State Thomas Jefferson, to assist him in furthering his political career. Although he had doubts about David's suitability, Jefferson approached the president with his petition and George Washington appointed him US Marshall of Virginia.[4]

While David was busy working the estate and building his political career, Molly ran their domestic life, overseeing the plantation house and its dependencies, supervising forty enslaved servants, and managing the household accounts. She and other women of her station had to acquire a wide array of skills to undertake such a formidable role successfully, including mastering intimate knowledge of food production, preservation, preparation, and presentation. This was necessary not only to feed a growing family—she gave birth to eight children, four of whom reached adulthood—but also to entertain family, friends, politicians, and dignitaries, including the occasional French nobleman. In the day-to-day oper-

Charles Balthazar Julien Fevrét de Saint-Mémin (French 1770–1852), Mrs. David Meade Randolph, *Richmond or Philadelphia, 1807, Library of Congress, Prints and Photographs Division, Washington, DC.*

Charles Balthazar Julien Fevrét de Saint-Mémin (French 1770–1852), David Meade Randolph, *Richmond or Philadelphia, 1807, Library of Congress, Prints and Photographs Division, Washington, DC.*

ations, enslaved cooks performed the actual cooking, but Molly supervised, instructing them in the recipes and closely inspecting their work.[5] She explained, "If the mistress of the family will every morning examine minutely, the different departments of her household, she must detect errors in their infant state, when they can be corrected with ease."[6] Hospitality was a hallmark of Antebellum Virginia society and it needed to appear effortless. Mary Randolph was a master.

While Presqu'île was an excellent training ground for honing the skills that served Molly well, life there was difficult. The 750-acre plantation was located near the confluence of the Appomattox and James rivers and much of the land consisted of hardwood swamp. La Rouchfoucauld noted during his stay that "the swampy grounds," produced an "abundance of noxious exhalations which prove a source of frequent and dangerous diseases. Mr. Randolph is himself very sickly; and his young and amiable wife has not enjoyed one month of good health since she first came to live on this plantation." David confessed to the duke that he wanted to sell Presqu'île and move into Richmond, where he had "frequent business in consequence of his office. . . ."[7]

The family moved to the capital in 1798 and there built a large house on the corner of Main and Fifth streets. Local merchant E. W. Roote dubbed the home "Moldavia," combining Molly and David's names.[8] The Randolphs lived lavishly, sparing no expense. They summered in Newport, Rhode Island, and while there hired the future Unitarian minister and reformer William Ellery Channing to tutor their children. People noted that the household at Moldavia was by no means "an economical one."[9] The Randolph's new home became a center of society as they entertained frequently and generously. Utilizing the arts she perfected at Presqu'île, Molly soon became acclaimed for serving excellent fare and providing stimulating conversation. Teacher and author Samuel Mordecai praised her as "one of the remark-

"Moldavia," Richmond, Virginia. Mary and David Randolph built the core of the house in 1800 on the corner of Main and Fifth streets. Joseph Gallego purchased the home from them in 1805 and added an addition and the double portico. Merchant John Allan bought the home at auction in 1825 and his young ward, sixteen-year-old Edgar Allan Poe, lived there briefly before leaving to attend the University of Virginia. The house was demolished in 1890. Photo courtesy of the Edgar Allan Poe Museum, Richmond.

able and distinguished persons of her day."[10]

The fame of Molly's culinary skills quickly spread beyond Richmond's elite. Two years after they arrived, Virginia's capital was rocked by the discovery of a planned slave rebellion led by a literate enslaved blacksmith named Gabriel. Gabriel intended to launch his assault August 30, 1800, but some of the participants revealed the plans before they could be implemented and Gabriel and twenty-five of his confederates were arrested and hanged. No white resident was to be spared in Gabriel's assault, with one exception. Purportedly, Mary Randolph was not to be harmed, so that she could cook for him.[11]

While Moldavia was noted as a center for social events, it also became a meeting place for political activities. As the first political parties began to form in the new republic, David's leanings put him in the

Federalist camp, in stark contrast to the politics of his cousin Thomas Jefferson. The two found themselves increasingly on opposite sides in political debates, straining family ties, even though Jefferson's daughter Martha married Molly's brother Thomas Mann Randolph, Jr. in 1790. David continued to serve as US Marshall through the Washington and Adams administrations, but that changed once Jefferson assumed the office in 1801. The new president felt he had no choice but to remove his cousin from his federal job, although Jefferson was cognizant of the strain it would bring to the family. He wrote his son-in-law March 12, 1801, acknowledging the action would cause him pain.[12] Jefferson dismissed his cousin, accusing him of packing a jury with Federalists during a lawsuit against pamphleteer James T. Callender, a charge David denied for the rest of his life.[13]

The breach in the family caused by David's dismissal grew rancorous and David and Molly were not shy in placing blame. David's rhetoric became increasingly antagonistic in his criticism of Jefferson's policies. And Molly was not afraid to join in the fray. Anglo-Irish émigré Harman Blennerhassett, an associate of Aaron Burr, spent an evening in Molly's company at a Richmond residence one Sunday in October 1807. Molly impressed him with her demeanor and "acute penetration," and Blennerhassett found she was quite blunt in expressing her opinions, describing her as,

> *a middle-aged lady, and very accomplished; of charming manners, and possessing a masculine mind. From this lady, the near relation of the President, and whose brother is married to his daughter, I heard more pungent strictures upon Jefferson's head and heart, because they were better*

founded than any I had ever heard be-
fore, and she certainly uttered more
treason than my wife ever dreamed
of. . . .[14]

Molly even helped spread reports about her cousin's relationship with his enslaved servant, Sally Hemings.[15]

The loss of David's government job was a blow for the Randolphs financially, but their situation grew increasingly desperate with the collapse of tobacco prices and an economic recession.[16] The results were devastating and the family was forced to econo mize. David sold Presqu'île and his other plantation holdings, but with depressed land prices, it was not enough. He sold lots he owned in Richmond and finally had to part with Moldavia itself in 1805. He even had to sell his prized horse. The family moved into a rented home on Cary Street. To earn money, David became a partner in a coal mining operation near Richmond called Black Heath and patented techniques he invented for boot and shoe manufacturing and carriage construction. By 1808, David had moved to Britain, where he spent the next years studying coal mining operations in Northern England and Wales and trying to stir up interest in his inventions among potential investors.[17] The family feud continued for decades. In a letter he wrote to Jefferson in 1815 after returning home to Virginia, David stated his feelings in clear terms:

The ruin of my family and the conse-
quent wretchedness of my declining
years, produced by an exercise of
arbitrary power in your hands, togeth-
er with the active malignity of certain
advocates of your infallibility, should
have been born with consistent resig-
nation, were it not that an unoffend-

ing hapless offspring are likely to be deprived of their only inheritance,— their fathers unsullied reputation.[18]

But finally, David healed the breach in 1823 when he testified for Jefferson during a lawsuit.[19]

In the meantime, when her husband went abroad, Molly took a bold step to support her family in their dire circumstances. According to Samuel Mordecai, "Mrs. R., who lacked neither energy nor industry, determined to open a boarding-house, feeling assured that those who had, in her prosperity, partaken of her hospitality, would second her exertions, when in adversity."[20] In 1808 she placed an advertisement that appeared in the March 4 issue of *The Richmond Virginia Gazette and General Advertiser*, stating, "Mrs. Randolph, Has established a Boarding House in Cary street, for the accommodation of Ladies and Gentlemen. She has comfortable chambers and a stable well supplied for a few horses."[21] It was unusual for a woman of her station to work supporting her family, but Molly felt that her friends would stand by her. She could select her customers carefully, and as there was a demand for excellent accommodations in Richmond, particularly when the General Assembly was in session, she could acquire a good clientele. Martha Jefferson Randolph wrote her father that "Sister Randolph" had managed to hold on to her house servants only by having taken out a mortgage previously, and she worried that Molly's new venture was doomed to fail because she "has not a single boarder yet." Martha feared her sister-in-law's fortunes were continuing to decline, that, "The ruin of the family is still extending itself daily."[22] But Molly's confidence in her friends was not misplaced and Richmond society flocked to support her in the new venture. Indeed, E. W. Roote, the same friend who had named Molly's home, "now conferred on her the title of Queen, and aided in enlisting subjects for her new realm."[23] The name may have originated from the story of Gabriel wanting to make Molly his queen.[24] In any case, according to Samuel Mordecai, "The Queen soon attracted as many of her subjects as her dominions could accommodate, and a loyal set they generally were. There were few more festive boards than the Queen's. Wit, humour and good-fellowship prevailed, but excess rarely. Social evenings were also enjoyed, and discord never intruded."[25]

Molly ran her boardinghouse in at least two different locations from 1807 until 1819. David, upon his return from Britain in 1815, continued his interest in inventing and filed patents for improvements in shipbuilding and candle making.[26] But as both were growing older, they decided to move to Washington, DC, to the home of their son William Beverly Randolph. There they lived a relatively quiet life, although they enjoyed being in close proximity to their cousins George Washington Parke Custis (Martha Washington's grandson and George's adopted son) and his wife Mary Ann Randolph Fitzhugh Custis across the Potomac River at their home in Arlington. Molly became godmother to their daughter Mary Ann Randolph Custis, who married a promising young Army officer from another old Virginia family, Robert E. Lee. David continued to invent and spent time at Arlington developing a compound to waterproof the house.[27] Meanwhile, Molly worked on a project of her own. She decided to publish her recipes.

Cottage Pie

Chapter 2

MEATS, FISH, POULTRY, ETC.

BEEF.

 ## BEEF A-LA-MODE.

TAKE the bone from a round of beef, fill the space with a forcemeat made of the crumbs of a stale loaf, four ounces of marrow, two heads of garlic chopped with thyme and parsley, some nutmeg, cloves, pepper and salt, mix it to a paste with the yelks of four eggs beaten, stuff the lean part of the round with it, and make balls of the remainder; sew a fillet of strong linen wide enough to keep it round and compact, put it in a vessel just sufficiently large to hold it, add a pint of red wine, cover it with sheets of tin or iron, set it in a brick oven properly heated, and bake it three hours; when done, skim the fat from the gravy, thicken it with brown flour, add some mushroom and walnut catsup, and serve it up garnished with forcemeat balls fried. It is still better when eaten cold with sallad.

French Pot Roast

SERVES 6

The main differences between a typical American pot roast and French pot roast are the types of herbs added and the use of wine instead of water in roasting. Boeuf à la Mode *appeared on French restaurant menus during the eighteenth century. Unlike Mushroom Catsup, Walnut Catsup is no longer available commercially. However, a close modern substitute is A-1 Steak Sauce.*

4 pounds boneless roast, round, or rump

1 beef bouillon cube

2 cups bread crumbs

12 cloves garlic, crushed

1 teaspoon thyme

1 tablespoon dried parsley flakes, or 2 tablespoons minced fresh parsley

½ teaspoon nutmeg

½ teaspoon ground cloves

½ teaspoon pepper

1 teaspoon salt

4 egg yolks, beaten

1 tablespoon butter

2 cups red wine

1 tablespoon flour

1 tablespoon Mushroom Catsup (see page 156), may substitute Worcestershire sauce

1 tablespoon Walnut Catsup (see page 158), may substitute A-1 Steak Sauce

Trim excess fat from the roast and butterfly it.

Dissolve the bouillon in 1 cup hot water. Combine it with bread crumbs, spices, and egg yolks.

Fill the roast with the stuffing. Roll it into a tube and secure it end-to-end with cooking twine.

In a large roasting pan over medium-high heat, brown the roast in the butter on all sides. Shape remaining stuffing into balls and fry, then set aside.

Preheat oven to 300°F.

Place roast in a baking pan, and pour the wine over it. Cover and bake for 3 hours, or until the meat is fork tender. Baste with its juices each hour during roasting.

Remove the roast from the pan and set aside.

To make the gravy, add 1 tablespoon of flour to the juices in the pan and stir over low heat until gravy thickens. Stir in the Mushroom and Walnut Catsups. Serve warm.

BRISKET OF BEEF BAKED.

BONE a brisket of beef, and make holes in it with a sharp knife about an inch apart, fill them alternately with fat bacon, parsley and oysters, all chopped small and seasoned with pounded cloves and nutmeg, pepper and salt, dredge it well with flour, lay it in a pan with a pint of red wine and a large spoonful of lemon pickle; bake it three hours, take the fat from the gravy and strain it; serve it up garnished with green pickles.

Beef Brisket

SERVES 6-8

Like pot roast, brisket is a less expensive cut of meat that can be tough if not cooked for a long period of time. Just as in Randolph's Beef a-la-Mode, her brisket recipe shows French influences with the use of wine.

2-3 slices bacon, chopped

1 (8-ounce) can oysters, chopped

½ teaspoon ground cloves

½ teaspoon nutmeg

½ teaspoon pepper

1 teaspoon salt

2-3 pounds beef brisket, boned

2 tablespoons flour

2 cups red wine

1 tablespoon Lemon Pickle (see page 155), may substitute zest of half a lemon

Preheat oven to 325°F.

In a bowl, mix the bacon, oysters, and spices together.

Cut pockets in the beef about 1 inch apart and fill with the oyster mixture.

Dredge meat in flour.

Place the brisket in an uncovered baking dish; pour the wine over it, and sprinkle with Lemon Pickle. Roast for 1 hour per pound, basting occasionally. The meat should be fork tender when cooked. Slice and serve.

BEEF OLIVES.

CUT slices from a fat rump of beef six inches long and half an inch thick, beat them well with a pestle; make a forcemeat of bread crumbs, fat bacon chopped, parsley, a little onion, some shred suet, pounded mace, pepper and salt; mix it up with the yelks of eggs, and spread a thin layer over each slice of beef, roll it up tight, and secure the rolls with skewers, set them before the fire, and turn them till they are a nice brown; have ready a pint of good gravy, thickened with brown flour and a spoonful of butter, a gill of red wine, with two spoonsful of mushroom catsup, lay the rolls in it, and stew them till tender; garnish with forcemeat balls.

Savory Beef Olives

SERVES 6-8

Olive was the word English cooks used to describe meats stuffed and served sliced with a sauce. These dishes developed in Britain by the sixteenth century.

3 pounds beef fillets

1 cup bread crumbs

½ pound diced bacon or ground pork

4 egg yolks, beaten

1 tablespoon dried parsley flakes or 2 tablespoons minced fresh parsley

1 onion, chopped

½ teaspoon mace

2 teaspoons salt

½ teaspoon pepper

3 tablespoons butter, divided

3 tablespoons flour, divided

2 cups beef broth

½ cup red wine

2 tablespoons Mushroom Catsup (see page 156), may substitute Worcestershire sauce

Pound fillets with a wooden mallet until very thin.

Mix bread crumbs, bacon (or pork), egg yolks, and seasonings together. Spread a small amount on each fillet.

Roll the meat carefully around the stuffing; tie or skewer securely. In a large pan, over medium-high heat, melt 2 tablespoons of butter. Brown beef olives, turning frequently. Remove beef from pan.

In the same pan, melt remaining 1 tablespoon butter and stir in 1 tablespoon flour. Stir in the beef broth, wine, and Mushroom Catsup until well blended.

Return the fillets to pan, cover, and simmer for 40 to 45 minutes or until meat is tender.

To make a sauce, remove the olives from the pan and set aside. Mix remaining 2 tablespoons of flour with some of the liquid in the pan and add back into the pan, stirring until thickened.

Cut and remove strings, and slice olives into medallions. Serve with the sauce either drizzled over the medallions or on the side.

A NICE LITTLE DISH OF BEEF.

MINCE cold roast beef, fat and lean, very fine, add chopped onion, pepper, salt, and a little good gravy, fill scollop shells two parts full, and fill them up with potatos mashed smooth with cream, put a bit of butter on the top, and set them in an oven to brown.

Cottage Pie

SERVES 6-8

Large scallop shells have been used as baking dishes for centuries, and are readily available at kitchen stores or through the Internet. An alternative is to use small, individual baking dishes.

2 cups cooked roast beef, minced, or 1 pound ground beef, browned

1 medium onion, diced

2 cups beef broth

2 tablespoons flour

4 medium potatoes, diced

⅓ cup whole milk

½ teaspoon salt

¼ teaspoon pepper

6 to 8 tablespoons butter

Combine beef, onions, and broth in a large skillet or Dutch oven over medium-high heat and simmer for 5 minutes. Remove the beef and onions with a slotted spoon and set aside. Reduce the heat to medium-low, and blend flour into the broth, continuing to stir until the gravy thickens. Return the beef and onions to pan and stir well.

Pour the beef mixture into greased individual baking dishes or onto baking scallop shells, filling them half full.

Preheat oven to 350°F.

Boil potatoes in enough water to cover until tender, then drain. Mash the potatoes, adding milk, salt, and pepper. Spoon the potatoes into the baking dishes atop the beef mixture. Top each with a pat of butter and bake until tops are golden brown, about 15 to 20 minutes.

VEAL.

VEAL CUTLETS
FROM THE FILLET OR LEG.

CUT off the flank and take the bone out, then take slices the size of the fillet and half an inch thick, beat two yelks of eggs light, and have some grated bread mixed with pepper, salt, pounded nutmeg and chopped parsley; beat the slices a little, lay them on a board and wash the upper side with the egg, cover it thick with the bread crumbs, press them on with a knife, and let them stand to dry a little, that they may not fall off in frying, then turn them gently, put egg and crumbs on in the same manner, put them into a pan of boiling lard, and fry them a light brown; have some good gravy ready, season it with a tea-spoonful of curry powder, a large one of wine, and one of lemon pickle, thicken with butter and brown flour, drain every drop of lard from the cutlets, lay them in the gravy, and stew them fifteen or twenty minutes, serve them up garnished with lemon cut in thin slices.

Veal Cutlets

SERVES 8

Randolph's use of curry spices is one of the more intriguing aspects of her cooking. Queen Elizabeth I granted a royal charter to the East India Company in 1600 and the British presence in India spread throughout the seventeenth and eighteenth centuries. Randolph may have been introduced to curry through some recipes included in British author Hannah Glasse's Art of Cookery Made Plain and Easy, first published in 1747. But she incorporated it into a number of her own recipes in unusual and innovative ways.

2 pounds veal cut from the leg

2 egg yolks

Salt and pepper, to taste

1 cup fine bread crumbs

½ teaspoon nutmeg

2 tablespoons dried parsley flakes or 2 tablespoons minced fresh parsley

1 cup flour, plus 1 tablespoon for gravy

2 tablespoons butter

1 cup whole milk

1 teaspoon Randolph's Spice Blend (see page 160) or curry powder

1 tablespoon red wine

1 tablespoon Lemon Pickle (see page 155), may substitute zest of half a lemon

8 thin lemon slices

Ask your butcher to bone and slice veal into 8 cutlets. Beat each cutlet with a wooden mallet until almost wafer thin.

In a small bowl, beat egg yolks with 1 tablespoon water, salt, and pepper.

In a separate bowl, mix the bread crumbs, nutmeg, and parsley together.

Put 1 cup flour on a plate for dredging. Coat each veal slice with flour, dip in the egg mixture, and then coat each side in bread crumbs.

Melt butter in a large skillet over medium-high heat and brown the cutlets in 2 or 3 batches. Transfer to paper towels to drain.

Add remaining 1 tablespoon flour to the skillet over medium-low heat and slowly add the milk, stirring to mix in all the browned bits left in the pan.

Mix the Spice Blend in 2 tablespoons of water and add it, along with the wine and Lemon Pickle, to the skillet.

Return the meat to the pan and simmer for 20 to 30 minutes until tender. Serve immediately, garnished with lemon slices.

VEAL CHOPS.

TAKE the best end of a rack of veal, cut it in chops, with one bone in each, leave the small end of the bone bare two inches, beat them flat, and prepare them with eggs and crumbs, as the cutlets, butter some half-sheets of white paper, wrap one round each chop, skewer it well, leaving the bare bone out, broil them till done, and take care the paper does not burn; have nice white sauce in a boat.

Veal Chops with White Sauce

SERVES 4

In seventeenth-century London, entrepreneurs began opening restaurants that specialized in serving individual portions of meat. They called them chophouses.

4 veal chops

2 egg yolks

Salt and pepper, to taste

1 cup fine bread crumbs

½ teaspoon nutmeg

2 tablespoons dried parsley flakes or 4 tablespoons minced fresh parsley

½ cup flour

For the White Sauce:
2 tablespoons flour

2 tablespoons butter, melted

1 cup milk

Beat chops with a wooden mallet to soften.

In a small bowl, beat the egg yolks with 1 tablespoon water and add salt and pepper.

In a separate bowl, mix the bread crumbs, nutmeg, and parsley together.

Coat each veal slice with flour, dip in the egg mixture, then coat each side with the bread crumb mixture. Line a baking sheet with parchment paper and place the chops on the paper. Season with salt and pepper.

Broil 6 to 7 minutes per side until browned. Serve with white sauce.

To make the White Sauce
While the veal chops are cooking, whisk together the flour and butter in a small saucepan; add the milk a little at a time, whisking to incorporate.

Bring to boil over medium-high heat, stirring constantly, until the sauce has thickened. You may add more milk for a thinner sauce.

SCOTCH COLLOPS OF VEAL.

THEY may be made of the nice part of the rack, or cut from the fillet, rub a little salt and pepper on them, and fry them a light brown; have a rich gravy seasoned with wine, and any kind of catsup you choose, with a few cloves of garlic, and some pounded mace, thicken it, put the collops in and stew them a short time, take them out, strain the gravy over, and garnish with bunches of parsley fried crisp, and thin slices of middling of bacon, curled around a skewer and boiled.

Scotch Collops

SERVES 4

Scotch Collops is a traditional Scottish meat dish made from either beef, veal, lamb, or venison. The word collop *means a thin slice of meat. In fifteenth-century England it became synonymous with bacon.*

½ cup butter, divided

1½ pounds veal, cut in 4 slices

2 cloves garlic, crushed

¼ cup flour

¼ teaspoon mace

2 cups beef broth

1 tablespoon red wine

1 tablespoon Mushroom Catsup (see page 156), may substitute Worcestershire sauce

Fresh parsley for garnish

2 tablespoons bacon bits (optional for garnish)

Melt half the butter in a large skillet over medium-high heat and lightly brown the veal on both sides. Transfer to a paper towel–lined plate and set aside.

Add the remaining butter to the skillet and sauté the garlic over medium heat. Stir in the flour and mace until smooth. Add the broth, wine, and Mushroom Catsup, and stir until the gravy thickens.

Return the veal to the skillet, reduce the heat to low, and simmer until the meat is cooked to desired doneness.

Garnish with parsley and bacon bits if desired.

RAGOUT OF
A BREAST OF VEAL.

SEPARATE the joints of the brisket, and saw off the sharp ends of the ribs, trim it neatly, and half roast it; put it in a stew pan with a quart of good gravy seasoned with wine, walnut and mushroom catsup, a tea-spoonful of curry powder, and a few cloves of garlic; stew it till tender, thicken the gravy, and garnish with sweatbreads nicely broiled.

Veal Ragout

SERVES 6

Ragouts are French stews that took Britain by storm. In 1731 Tom Jones *author Henry Fielding authored a satire decrying the state of the British Army, blaming its decline on soldiers eating French dishes instead of the more patriotic* Roast Beef of Old England.

⅓ cup butter

2 pounds stew veal, cut in small pieces

2 cups wine

½ cup Mushroom Catsup (see page 156), may substitute Worcestershire sauce

½ cup Walnut Catsup (see page 158), may substitute A1 Steak Sauce

1 teaspoon Randolph's Spice Blend (see page 160) or curry powder

2 cloves garlic, crushed

Salt and pepper, to taste

1 tablespoon flour

In a large skillet or Dutch oven, melt the butter and brown the veal on both sides. Stir in the wine, catsups, spice blend, garlic, and salt and pepper. Add enough water to cover the meat and stir. Cook over low heat for 30 to 40 minutes, until tender.

In a small bowl, mix the flour with an equal amount of sauce. Stir this paste into the sauce and cook 3 to 4 minutes to thicken. Serve immediately.

FORCEMEAT BALLS.

TAKE half a pound of veal, and half a pound of suet cut fine, and beat in a marble mortar or wooden bowl; add a few sweet herbs shred fine, a little mace pounded fine, a small nutmeg grated, a little lemon peel, some pepper and salt, and the yelks of two eggs; mix them well together, and make them into balls and long pieces—then roll them in flour, and fry them brown. If they are for the use of white sauce, do not fry them, but put them in a sauce-pan of hot water and let them boil a few minutes.

Forcemeat

Forcemeat is an ancient food appearing in Imperial Roman recipes as early as the fourth or fifth century. Randolph uses forcemeat in a number of her recipes, either as a stuffing or as a garnish in the form of meatballs. However, she also uses the word forcemeat *when talking about bread stuffings. A good substitute for forcemeat is a mild sausage.*

½ pound veal, ground

½ pound suet

2 egg yolks

1 teaspoon parsley

1 teaspoon basil

1½ teaspoons salt

½ teaspoon nutmeg

⅛ teaspoon mace

Zest of half a lemon

½ teaspoon pepper

½ cup flour

2 tablespoons cooking oil

Blend the veal and suet in a food processor. Mix in all remaining ingredients except for flour and oil and blend until well combined.

For Forcemeat balls, shape by teaspoonful into balls, roll in flour, and fry in skillet with cooking oil over medium-high heat until brown on all sides.

TO MAKE A PIE OF
SWEETBREADS AND OYSTERS.

BOIL the sweetbreads tender, stew the oysters, season them with pepper and salt, and thicken with cream, butter, the yelks of eggs and flour, put a puff paste at the bottom and around the sides of a deep dish, take the oysters up with an egg spoon, lay them in the bottom, and cover them with the sweetbreads, fill the dish with gravy, put a paste on the top, and bake it. This is the most delicate pie that can be made. The sweetbread of veal is the most delicious part, and may be broiled, fried, or dressed in any way, and is always good.

Sweetbread and Oyster Pie

SERVES 6

Sweetbread is organ meat from the thymus and pancreas. The key to preparing any recipe calling for sweetbreads is soaking them in water first. This removes any musty flavor usually associated with other organ meats like liver and kidney. Although Randolph doesn't call for it in her recipe, adding lemon juice during cooking also helps remove any unpleasant taste.

1 pound sweetbreads, may substitute veal, cut into 1-inch cubes

2 teaspoons salt, divided

4 tablespoons lemon juice

½ pint oysters

½ teaspoon pepper

1 cup cream

½ cup butter

Puff Pastry (see page 171)

Soak the sweetbreads in cold water for 1 hour. (Veal does not need to be soaked.)

In a large saucepot or stockpot, bring 2 quarts water to boil with 1 teaspoon of salt and lemon juice.

Drain the sweetbreads and use a slotted spoon to place them carefully in the boiling water. Boil for 15 to 20 minutes, then remove to drain on paper towels.

In a separate pot over medium heat, stew the oysters in their liquor just until they curl. Stir in the remaining 1 teaspoon salt, pepper, cream, and butter. Remove from heat.

Preheat oven to 350°F.

Line a pan with the puff pastry. Spoon the oysters onto the pastry and arrange the meat atop the oysters. Pour the oyster sauce over that and top with the other pastry, pinching the sides to seal. Bake for 40 minutes, or until the crust is golden brown.

LAMB.

 ## BAKED LAMB.

CUT the shank bone from a hind-quarter, separate the joints of the loin, lay it in a pan with the kidney uppermost, sprinkle some pepper and salt, add a few cloves of garlic, a pint of water and a dozen large ripe tomatoes with the skins taken off, bake it but do not let it be burnt, thicken the gravy with a little butter and brown flour.

Baked Lamb with Tomatoes

SERVES 4-6

An easy trick to peeling tomatoes is to take a knife and score a shallow cross on the bottom of each tomato. Then set a pot of water to boil and fill a bowl with water and ice cubes. Blanch each tomato for two to three minutes and immediately dunk them into the ice water to stop them from cooking. The skin at the cross will be peeled away and easy to remove from the rest of the tomato.

1 (2- to 2½-pound) loin roast

Salt and pepper, to taste

2 cloves garlic, crushed

12 small tomatoes, peeled or 1 (32-ounce) can peeled tomatoes

1 tablespoon flour

Preheat oven to 325°F.

Place the roast in a roasting pan and sprinkle with salt and pepper. Add 2 cups water and the garlic. Surround the roast with the peeled tomatoes, cover, and roast 25 to 30 minutes per pound.

Remove the roast from the pan and set aside.

In a cup or bowl, mix the flour with 1 tablespoon of the pan juices to make a paste, then add the flour paste to the pan, stir and cook 3 to 4 minutes to make gravy. Slice on the diagonal, cover with gravy, and serve immediately.

MUTTON.

 BAKED LEG OF MUTTON.

TAKE the flank off, but leave all the fat, cut out the bone, stuff the place with a rich forcemeat, lard the top and sides with bacon, put it in a pan with a pint of water, some chopped onion and cellery cut small, a gill of red wine, one of mushroom catsup and a tea-spoonful of curry powder, bake it and serve it up with the gravy, garnish with forcemeat balls fried.

Stuffed Leg of Mutton

SERVES 8

Because it has a higher fat content than lamb, mutton has a stronger, richer flavor similar to game meat.

1 (5-pound) leg of mutton, boned

1 pound Forcemeat (see page 59), may substitute mild pork sausage

½ pound bacon, cut into small pieces

1 onion, chopped

½ cup celery, chopped

½ cup red wine

½ cup Mushroom Catsup (see page 156), may substitute Worcestershire sauce

1 teaspoon Randolph's Spice Blend (see page 160) or curry powder

1 tablespoon flour

Preheat oven to 300°F.

Prepare the Forcemeat and stuff it into the bone cavity of the leg of mutton. Tie or skewer securely closed. Make cuts all over the leg and stuff each hole with a piece of uncooked bacon.

Place the leg in a roasting pan with 2 cups water and all remaining ingredients except flour. Bake covered for 30 minutes per pound until the meat is fork tender.

Remove leg from pan and set aside.

Mix the flour with 1 tablespoon of the sauce to make a paste, then add this back to the pan, stir and cook 3 to 4 minutes to thicken the gravy. Serve immediately.

TO HARRICO MUTTON.

TAKE the nicest part of the rack, divide it into chops, with one bone in each, beat them flat, sprinkle salt and pepper on them, and broil them nicely; make a rich gravy out of the inferior parts, season it well with pepper, a little spice, and any kind of catsup you choose; when sufficiently done, strain it, and thicken it with butter and brown flour, have some carrots and turnips cut into small dice and boiled till tender, put them in the gravy, lay the chops in and stew them fifteen minutes; serve them up garnished with green pickle.

Haricot Mutton

SERVES 4

Haricot is meat stewed with root vegetables. Slow cooked, it was an ideal one-pot meal for the common people. Haricot Mutton recipes can be traced back in England to as early as 1611. Ask your butcher to divide the rack into chops.

1 (8-bone) rack of mutton, divided into chops

2 tablespoons butter

1 tablespoon flour

1 teaspoon salt

½ teaspoon pepper

1 tablespoon Mushroom Catsup (see page 156), may substitute Worcestershire sauce

1 cup carrots, diced

1 cup turnips, diced

Wash and dry the chops and brown them in butter in a large skillet over medium-high heat.

Preheat oven to 425°F.

Place the skillet in oven (if it has oven proof handle, otherwise transfer chops to a roasting pan). Bake the chops for 10 minutes, then turn them over and bake for another 10 minutes.

Set the chops aside while you make the gravy.

Add flour to the skillet drippings and stir to create a gravy, adding water if necessary. Stir in salt, pepper, and Mushroom Catsup.

In a large saucepan over high heat, bring 2 quarts water to boil. Add the vegetables and boil for 10 minutes until tender. Drain.

Stir the vegetables into the gravy and return the chops to the skillet. Bake an additional 10 minutes and then serve immediately.

PORK.

 ## TO BARBECUE SHOTE.

THIS is the name given in the southern states to a fat young hog, which, when the head and feet are taken off, and it is cut into four quarters, will weigh six pounds per quarter. Take a fore-quarter, make several incisions between the ribs, and stuff it with rich forcemeat; put it in a pan with a pint of water, two cloves of garlic, pepper, salt, two gills of red wine, and two of mushroom catsup, bake it, and thicken the gravy with batter and brown flour; it must be jointed, and the ribs cut across before it is cooked; or it cannot be carved well; lay it in the dish with the ribs uppermost; if it be not sufficiently brown, add a little burnt sugar to the gravy, garnish with balls.

Stuffed Barbeque Pork Shoulder

SERVES 8-10

Anthropologists believe humans and their ancestors have been cooking meat for around one million years, and that cooking with fire was key to the evolution of homo sapiens.

1 (4-pound) boned pork shoulder roast or Boston Butt

1 pound Forcemeat (see page 59), may substitute mild pork sausage

1 cup red wine

1 cup Mushroom Catsup (see page 156), may substitute Worcestershire sauce

2 cloves garlic

Salt and pepper, to taste

2 tablespoons butter

2 tablespoons whole flour

2 teaspoons Kitchen Bouquet, optional

Remove the roast from the refrigerator at least 30 minutes before cooking to bring to room temperature.

Preheat oven to 450°F

Open the pork roast to where bone was removed and fill with Forcemeat. If it has been rolled, you may need to butterfly it before stuffing. Secure the roast with cooking twine and place in a baking pan.

In a bowl, stir together 2 cups water, the wine, Mushroom Catsup, garlic, salt, and pepper, and pour over the roast.

Roast for 15 minutes, then reduce heat to 350°F. Bake 2 hours more, basting every 15 minutes, and adding water as needed to cover ingredients. The meat is done when it is fork tender. Remove the roast from the pan and set aside.

In a separate pan, melt the butter and stir in the flour to make a paste. On the stovetop over low heat, add the paste to the juices left in the roasting pan, and stir until the mixture thickens into a sauce. If needed, brown with Kitchen Bouquet.

Remove the twine from pork. Slice the pork and serve with the sauce in a separate container.

LEG OF PORK WITH PEASE PUDDING.

BOIL a small leg of pork that has been sufficiently salted, score the top and serve it up; the pudding must be in a separate dish; get small delicate pease, wash them well, and tie them in a cloth, allowing a little room for swelling, boil them with the pork, then mash and season them, tie them up again and finish boiling it; take care not to break the pudding in turning it out.

Roasted Pork with Pease Pudding

SERVES 8

Many people will be familiar with the nursery rhyme, "Pease Porridge Hot." This originates from the Middle English "pease pottage," a savory dish of boiled legumes also known as pease pudding, frequently used in English cooking to accompany pork.

For the Roasted Pork:

4 pounds pork leg

2 teaspoons salt

For the Pease Pudding:

1 pound, or 2 cups, dried green split peas

¼ pound bacon

Salt and pepper

Preheat oven to 450°F.

In a large saucepan, boil 2 quarts water.

Place the pork in colander in the sink and pour the boiling water over it to scald the entire surface. Pat dry. Place pork leg in a baking dish and rub it overall with salt.

Bake for 15 minutes, then reduce the heat to 350°F and continue to bake for 2 hours, until the meat is fork tender.

In a separate large pot over high heat, boil 1 quart water. Add the peas and bacon, reduce the heat to low, and simmer 1 hour, or until the peas are soft.

Remove the bacon and discard. Mash the peas. Salt and pepper them to taste. To mold, fill a bowl with the peas and let them rest 10 minutes, then invert onto a serving platter.

Serve separately or together with the pork leg on a platter.

SEA PIE

LAY at the bottom of a small Dutch oven some slices of boiled pork or salt beef, then potatos and onions cut in slices, salt, pepper, thyme and parsley shred fine, some crackers soaked, and a layer of fowls cut up, or slices of veal; cover them with a paste not too rich, put another layer of each article, and cover them with paste until the oven is full; put a little butter between each layer, pour in water till it reaches the top crust, to which you must add wine, catsup of any kind you please, and some pounded cloves; let it stew until there is just gravy enough left; serve it in a deep dish and pour the gravy on.

TO MAKE PASTE FOR THE PIE.

POUR half a pound of butter or dripping, boiling hot, into a quart of flour, add as much water as will make it a paste, work it, and roll it well before you use it. It is quite a savoury paste.

A SEA PIE

SERVES 4

Ironically, Sea Pie is not a fish dish, but rather a meat dish that was easy to prepare for sailors at sea using dried or salted meats.

1 cup flour

2 tablespoons butter

½ pound pork or beef, cut in cubes

½ pound fowl or veal, cut in cubes

4 potatoes, peeled and diced

1 medium onion, thinly sliced

1 teaspoon salt

¼ teaspoon pepper

½ teaspoon thyme

1 tablespoon dried parsley flakes or 2 tablespoons minced fresh parsley

½ teaspoon ground cloves

¼ cup red wine

¼ cup Mushroom Catsup (see page 156), may substitute Worcestershire sauce

2 pie crusts (see recipe below, or use store-bought)

Place the flour in a shallow dish.

Melt the butter in a large skillet or Dutch oven over medium-high heat.

Roll meat cubes in the flour and brown them in the butter, turning to brown all sides. Add enough water to cover the meat, lower the heat to medium-low, and simmer for 1 hour.

Add the vegetables and seasonings and continue to cook for 30 minutes, or until the vegetables are tender. Stir in the wine and catsup.

Preheat oven to 350°F.

Line 9-inch pie plate or baking dish with a pie crust and bake for 15 minutes.

Remove the crust from the oven and fill with the meat and vegetables.

Cover with the second crust. Return to the oven and bake for 20 minutes, or until the crust is golden brown.

Double Pastry Shell

MAKES 2 9-INCH CRUSTS

½ pound cold butter

2½ cups flour

½ teaspoon salt

In a large bowl, blend together butter, flour, and salt. Gradually add chilled water (6–8 tablespoons) until dough holds together. Divide in half and roll out on a floured surface to size of the baking dish.

FISH.

 ## TO BAKE STURGEON.

GET a piece of sturgeon with the skin on, the piece next to the tail, scrape it well, cut out the gristle, and boil it about twenty minutes to take out the oil; take it up, pull off the large scales, and when cold, stuff it with forcemeat, made of bread crumbs, butter, chopped parsley, pepper and salt, put it in a Dutch oven just large enough to hold it, with a pint and a half of water, a gill of red wine, one of mushroom catsup, some salt and pepper, stew it gently till the gravy is reduced to the quantity necessary to pour over it; take up your sturgeon carefully, thicken the gravy with a spoonful of butter rubbed into a large one of brown flour—see that it is perfectly smooth when you put it in the dish.

Baked Sturgeon

SERVES 4

Sturgeon can be purchased in local fish markets or online, but if you find it unavailable or need a ready substitute, denser meat-like fishes such as halibut, mahi mahi, and swordfish work well.

1 (2-pound) sturgeon

4 cups bread crumbs

½ cup whole milk

3 tablespoons butter, divided

¼ teaspoon salt

Dash pepper

Dash nutmeg

½ cup Mushroom Catsup (see page 156), may substitute Worcestershire sauce

½ cup white wine

1 tablespoon flour

Wash thoroughly, debone, and remove the skin from the fish.

Prepare the stuffing by soaking the bread crumbs in a bowl of milk for 15 minutes.

Pour the mixture into a saucepan and simmer on low heat until the liquid has evaporated, stirring constantly. Add 2 tablespoons butter and the spices and mix well.

Stuff the fish and place it in a Dutch oven. Add 3 cups water, the Mushroom Catsup, and wine. Salt and pepper to taste. Simmer on low for 8 to 10 minutes, until the fish is fork tender. Carefully remove the fish and set aside.

Add remaining 1 tablespoon butter and flour to the liquid in the Dutch oven, and stir over medium-low heat until it thickens into a sauce. Pour sauce over fish and serve immediately.

TO BAKE A SHAD.

THE shad is a very indifferent fish unless it be large and fat; when you get a good one, prepare it nicely, put some forcemeat inside, and lay it at full length in a pan with a pint of water, a gill of red wine, one of mushroom catsup, a little pepper, vinegar, salt, a few cloves of garlic, and six cloves: stew it gently till the gravy is sufficiently reduced; there should always be a fish-slice with holes to lay the fish on, for the convenience of dishing without breaking it; when the fish is taken up, slip it carefully into the dish; thicken the gravy with butter and brown flour, and pour over it.

Baked Shad

SERVES 6-8

Shad was an important staple for the people of Virginia since the arrival of Native Americans. A type of herring, the fish were plentiful in the Chesapeake Bay and rivers until overfishing and pollution took its toll. It is still available, but can be substituted with medium darker meat fish such as mullet, mackerel, and bluefish.

3–4 pounds shad, filleted and butterflied

Salt and pepper

1½ cups bread crumbs

1½ cups cornbread crumbs

1 medium onion, chopped

½ cup whole milk

8 tablespoons (1 stick) butter, room temperature, divided

½ cup red wine

½ cup Mushroom Catsup (see page 156), may substitute Worcestershire sauce

1 tablespoon white vinegar

3 cloves garlic, crushed

6 cloves

1 tablespoon flour

Preheat oven to 350°F.

Clean and wash the shad. Pat it dry and sprinkle both sides with salt and pepper.

Make a stuffing by combining both bread crumbs, onion, milk, and 4 tablespoons butter in a bowl. Stir well to combine.

Fill the shad with the stuffing and press the edges together. Place in a baking pan and cover with 2 cups water, the wine, Mushroom Catsup, vinegar, garlic, cloves, 1 teaspoon salt, and ½ teaspoon pepper. Bake for 1½ hours, basting frequently.

Transfer the fish to a serving platter. Skim the cloves from the sauce left in the baking pan and discard them.

Melt the remaining butter in a small pan and stir in flour to make a paste. Add this to the juices in the baking pan, and stir over low heat until the mixture thickens to a gravy. Pour gravy over fish and serve immediately.

TO FRY PERCH.

CLEAN the fish nicely, but do not take out the roes, dry them on a cloth, sprinkle some salt, and dredge them with flour, lay them separately on a board; when one side is dry, turn them, sprinkle salt and dredge the other side; be sure the lard boils when you put the fish in, and fry them with great care; they should be a yellowish brown when done. Send melted butter or anchovy sauce in a boat.

Fried Perch

SERVES 4

An extremely simple recipe, the addition of hot butter, or Randolph's more elaborate Anchovy Sauce (see page 97), turns these basic fried fish into a culinary delight.

2 pounds fillets of
  perch

1 teaspoon salt

1 cup flour

2 tablespoons
  shortening

Cut the fish in serving-size portions and sprinkle both sides with salt. Dredge the fish in flour.

Heat the shortening in a heavy frying pan over medium-high heat and fry the fillets for 5 minutes until brown, then carefully turn and cook until brown on the other side.

Serve hot with butter or Anchovy Sauce (see page 97).

TO MAKE A CURRY
OF CATFISH.

TAKE the white channel catfish, cut off their heads, skin and clean them, cut them in pieces four inches long, put as many as will be sufficient for a dish into a stew pan with a quart of water, two onions, and chopped parsley; let them stew gently till the water is reduced to half a pint, take the fish out and lay them on a dish, cover them to keep them hot, rub a spoonful of butter into one of flour, add a large tea-spoonful of curry powder, thicken the gravy with it, shake it over the fire a few minutes, and pour it over the fish; be careful to have the gravy smooth.

Curried Catfish

SERVES 4-6

Although a form of catfish curry developed in Indo-China, this recipe may be a Randolph original, applying her taste for curry spices to a powerfully flavored local fish.

1 large onion, coarsely chopped

1 tablespoon dried parsley flakes or ½ cup minced fresh parsley

1 tablespoon butter

2 pounds catfish, dressed, and cut in small pieces

1 tablespoon flour

1 teaspoon Randolph's Spice Blend (see page 160), or curry powder

Salt and pepper, to taste

In a large skillet over medium-high heat, sauté the onion and parsley in butter for 3 to 5 minutes. Add the pieces of fish and 1 cup water, and reduce the heat to medium-low. Simmer for 18 to 20 minutes.

Into 1 cup cold water, blend the flour and spice blend. Stir this into the skillet of fish and continue to simmer for 3 to 4 minutes, until thickened. Season with salt and pepper.

MATELOTE OF
ANY KIND OF FIRM FISH.

CUT the fish in pieces six inches long, put it in a pot with onion, parsley, thyme, mushrooms, a little spice, pepper and salt—add red wine and water enough for gravy, set it on a quick fire and reduce it one-third, thicken with a spoonful of butter and two of flour; put it in a dish with bits of bread fried in butter, and pour the gravy over it.

Fish in Wine Sauce

SERVES 6

Matelote French stew is different from its more famous cousin bouillabaisse, which is made using seafood. Walleye, trout, and other freshwater fish work well in this recipe.

1 tablespoon flour

1 tablespoon butter, melted

2 pounds freshwater fish, cut in small pieces

1 onion, chopped

½ cup mushrooms, sliced

½ cup red wine

1 tablespoon dried parsley flakes, or 2 tablespoons minced fresh parsley

½ teaspoon thyme

Salt and pepper, to taste

For the Croutons:
Small loaf stale bread, crusts removed

½ cup butter

Blend the flour and butter together in a small bowl and set aside.

Combine the fish and all remaining ingredients in a large pan with enough water to cover, and simmer over medium-low heat for 20 minutes, adding water as needed to cover ingredients.

Stir the flour and butter paste into the sauce over low heat until the sauce thickens.

Serve hot with croutons.

To make the Croutons
Cube bread into desired sizes.

Melt the butter in a frying pan and add bread. Fry until light brown. Drain on paper towels.

TO DRESS COD FISH.

BOIL the fish tender, pick it from the bones, take an equal quantity of Irish potatos, or parsnips boiled and chopped, and the same of onions well boiled; add a sufficiency of melted butter, some grated nutmeg, pepper, and salt, with a little brandy or wine; rub them in a mortar till well mixed; if too stiff, liquify it with cream or thickened milk, put paste in the bottom of a dish, pour in the fish, and bake it. For change, it may be baked in the form of patties.

Baked Cod and Mashed Potatoes

SERVES 4

1 pound cod

4 tablespoons butter, divided

Salt and pepper, to taste

½ cup white wine

¼ teaspoon nutmeg

1 cup mashed potatoes or parsnips

1 cup onion, chopped and boiled

Preheat oven to 400°F.

Grease a baking dish with 2 tablespoons butter.

Salt and pepper the fish to taste and place in the dish. Bake 15 minutes, until the fish is opaque and flakes easily.

In a bowl, mix all remaining ingredients together with the fish and blend well. If the mixture is too thick, thin it with a little whole milk or cream. Pour this mixture into the baking dish and broil 15 minutes, or until golden brown.

COD FISH PIE.

SOAK the fish, boil it and take off the skin, pick the meat from the bones, and mince it very fine; take double the quantity of your fish, of stale bread grated; pour over it as much new milk, boiling hot, as will wet it completely, add minced parsley, nutmeg, pepper, and made mustard, with as much melted butter as will make it sufficiently rich; the quantity must be determined by that of the other ingredients—beat these together very well, add the minced fish, mix it all, cover the bottom of the dish with good paste, pour the fish in, put on a lid and bake it.

Codfish Pie

SERVES 6

The history of America is inseparable from codfish. Native Americans feasted upon it as a staple. Europeans, beginning with the Vikings, sailed the North Atlantic to the Grand Banks, some of the richest fishing grounds in the world, and stopped on the shores of North America to dry and salt their catches before returning to Europe.

6 tablespoons butter, divided

2 pounds cod, filleted

Salt and pepper, to taste

1 tablespoon dried parsley flakes, or 2 tablespoons minced fresh parsley

Pinch nutmeg

1 teaspoon store-bought yellow mustard

1½ cups whole milk

Double pastry shell (see page 73)

Preheat oven to 400°F.

Grease a baking dish with 2 tablespoons butter.

Salt and pepper the fish and place in the dish. Bake for 15 minutes, until fish is opaque and flakes easily. Mince the fish.

Reduce the oven heat to 350°F.

In a saucepan, combine the fish, parsley, nutmeg, mustard, and milk over medium-low heat. Stir until thickened.

Prepare a double crust and line a 9-inch pie pan with one crust. Add filling and top with second crust.

Bake 20 minutes, or until top is golden brown. Serve immediately.

TO DRESS ANY KIND
OF SALTED FISH.

TAKE the quantity necessary for the dish, wash them, and lay them in fresh water for a night; then put them on the tin plate with holes, and place it in the fish kettle—sprinkle over it pounded cloves and pepper, with four cloves of garlic; put in a bundle of sweet herbs and parsley, a large spoonful of tarragon, and two of common vinegar, with a pint of wine; roll one quarter of a pound of butter in two spoonsful of flour, cut it in small pieces, and put it over the fish—cover it closely, and simmer it over a slow fire half an hour; take the fish out carefully, and lay it in the dish, set it over hot water, and cover it till the gravy has boiled a little longer—take out the garlic and herbs, pour it over the fish, and serve it up. It is very good when eaten cold with salad, garnished with parsley.

Dressed Salt Fish

SERVES 4

Cod is not the only fish that can be preserved, dried and salted, although it is the most common. Other fish frequently preserved that way include pollack, snapper, and even shark.

- 2 pounds salted fish fillets
- 2 cups white wine
- 2 tablespoons white wine vinegar
- ½ teaspoon ground cloves
- 4 cloves garlic, crushed
- 1 teaspoon basil
- 1 tablespoon parsley
- 2 tablespoons flour
- 4 tablespoons butter

Soak the fillets in water in a refrigerator overnight.

When you are ready to bake, remove fillets from water, pat dry, and arrange in a baking dish.

Preheat oven to 350°F.

Pour the wine and vinegar over the fish.

In a small bowl, stir together the cloves, garlic, basil, and parsley, and sprinkle this over the fish.

In a dish, cut together the flour and butter and sprinkle it over the fish.

Bake 15 minutes, or until the fish flakes easily.

Transfer the fish to a platter and keep warm while you heat the sauce, stirring, over medium heat to thicken.

May be served hot or cold with sauce on the side or poured over fish before serving.

TO STEW CARP.

GUT and scale your fish, wash and dry them well with a clean cloth, dredge them with flour, fry them in lard until they are a light brown, and then put them in a stew pan with half a pint of water, and half a pint of red wine, a meat spoonful of lemon pickle, the same of Walnut Catsup, a little mushroom powder and cayenne to your taste, a large onion stuck with cloves, and a slick of horse-radish; cover your pan close up to keep in the steam; let them stew gently over a stove fire, till the gravy is reduced to just enough to cover your fish in the dish; then take the fish out, and put them on the dish you intend for the table, set the gravy on the fire, and thicken it with flour, and a large lump of butter; boil it a little, and strain it over your fish; garnish them with pickled mushrooms and scraped horse-radish, and send them to the table.

Stewed Carp

SERVES 4

Carp is eaten in many parts of the world, but is not common in the United States. It is an oily fish with a very strong flavor that needs flavorful ingredients, thus Randolph's use of cayenne pepper, horseradish, and vinegar-based condiments. If carp is unavailable, good substitutes are bluefish, ocean perch, or bass.

1 tablespoon shortening

2 pounds carp, cleaned and cut into small pieces

1 cup flour, plus 1 tablespoon

1 cup red wine

2 tablespoons Lemon Pickle (see page 155), may substitute zest of a lemon

2 tablespoons Walnut Catsup (see page 158), may substitute A1 Steak Sauce

½ teaspoon cayenne pepper

1 tablespoon grated horseradish

1 large onion, chopped

1 teaspoon ground cloves

Salt and pepper, to taste

1 tablespoon butter, melted

Heat the shortening in a large skillet over medium-high heat.

Dredge the fish pieces in 1 cup flour and fry 5 minutes on each side, or until the fish is browned on both sides.

Add 1 cup water and all the remaining ingredients except for butter to the skillet. Reduce the heat to low and simmer gently until the fish is tender and flakes easily.

Use a slotted spoon to remove the fish to a casserole dish or a shallow bowl while you make the sauce.

In a cup or small bowl, stir the butter together with remaining 1 tablespoon flour. Add this paste to the skillet sauce and stir over medium-low heat until it thickens.

Pour the sauce over the fish and serve.

TO SCOLLOP OYSTERS.

WHEN the oysters are opened, put them in a bowl, and wash them out of their own liquor; put some in the scollop shells, strew over them a few bread crumbs, and lay a slice of butter on them, then more oysters, bread crumbs, and a slice of butter on the top; put them into a Dutch oven to brown, and serve them up in the shells.

Scalloped Oysters

SERVES 4

Scalloped oysters are traditionally served in Southern homes as a side dish at Thanksgiving and Christmas—in our household, on Christmas Eve. This new version of the recipe calls for baking the oysters in a single dish, although Randolph baked hers in individual scallop baking shells.

1 pint oysters

1 cup saltine cracker crumbs, divided into 3 portions

8 tablespoons (1 stick) butter

Preheat oven to 450°F.

Drain the oysters and discard the liquid. Cover the bottom of a baking dish with a layer of crumbs. Add a layer of oysters, and dot with half the butter. Repeat the process, ending with crumbs on top.

Bake for 20 to 30 minutes, until the top is crisp and golden brown.

TO MAKE OYSTER LOAVES.

TAKE little round loaves, cut off the tops, scrape out all the crumbs, then put the oysters into a stew pan with the crumbs that came out of the loaves, a little water, and a good lump of butter; stew them together ten or fifteen minutes, then put in a spoonful of good cream, fill your loaves, lay the bit of crust carefully on again, set them in the oven to crisp. Three are enough for a side dish.

Oyster Loaves

SERVES 4

Not to be confused with the New Orleans sandwich of the same name, oyster loaves were popular in the eighteenth and early nineteenth centuries because they could be carried easily for a lunch or picnic.

8 dinner buns or yeast rolls

1 (8-ounce) can oysters, or 1 pint fresh oysters, plus the liquor

½ cup butter

2 tablespoons cream

Salt and pepper, to taste

Preheat oven to 375°F.

Cut a thin slice off the top of each bun to make a lid. Scrape out the insides of the buns without cutting through, saving the bread crumbs.

In a saucepan over medium heat, combine these crumbs with the oysters, their liquor, butter, and cream.

Cook, stirring, just until the mixture has slightly thickened. Add salt and pepper to taste. Fill the buns with the oyster mixture and replace the tops.

Bake for 10 to 12 minutes, just long enough to heat through and brown the tops.

FISH SAUCE,
TO KEEP A YEAR.

CHOP twenty-four anchovies, bones and all, two shallots, a handful of scraped horse radish, four blades of mace, one quart of white wine, one pint of anchovy liquor, one pint of claret, twelve cloves, and twelve pepper corns; boil them together till reduced to a quart, then strain it off into a bottle for use Two spoonsful will be sufficient for a pound of butter.

Anchovy Sauce

MAKES APPROXIMATELY 2 CUPS

Similar to Mushroom Catsup, this style of Anchovy Sauce (not to be confused with Italian or Asian anchovy sauces) is still bottled by the G^{eo} Watkins Co. and is available at grocers in Great Britain or via the Internet. It is an excellent accompaniment to fried fish.

2 (2-ounce) cans anchovies, plus the liquid

1 shallot, minced

1 tablespoon prepared horseradish

¼ teaspoon mace

2 cups white wine

1 tablespoon anchovy paste

½ cup red wine

6 cloves

6 peppercorns

Drain the anchovies, retaining liquid, and mince.

Stir all ingredients, including the anchovy liquid, together in a saucepan and bring to boil over high heat, then reduce the heat to low and simmer 1 hour. Strain and bottle the liquid. This sauce will keep, refrigerated, for at least 3 months.

POULTRY, ETC.

 ## TO ROAST A TURKEY.

MAKE the forcemeat thus: take the crumb of a loaf of bread, a quarter of a pound of beef suet shred fine, a little sausage meat or veal scraped and pounded very fine, nutmeg, pepper, and salt to your taste; mix it lightly with three eggs, stuff the craw with it, spit it, and lay it down a good distance from the fire, which should be clear and brisk; dust and baste it several times with cold lard; it makes the froth stronger than basting it with the hot out of the dripping pan, and makes the turkey rise better; when it is enough, froth it up as before, dish it, and pour on the same gravy as for the boiled turkey, or bread sauce; garnish with lemon and pickles, and serve it up; if it be of a middle size, it will require one hour and a quarter to roast.

TO MAKE SAUCE FOR A TURKEY. [OYSTER]

AS you open the oysters, put a pint into a bowl, wash them out of their own liquor, and put them in another bowl; when the liquor has settled, pour it off into a sauce pan with a little white gravy, and a tea-spoonful of lemon pickle—thicken it with flour and a good lump of butter; boil it three or four minutes, put in a spoonful of good cream, add the oysters, keep shaking them over the fire till they are quite hot, but don't let them boil, for it will make them hard and appear small.

TO MAKE SAUCE FOR A TURKEY. [BREAD]

CUT the crumb of a loaf of bread in thin slices, and put it in cold water with a few pepper corns, a little salt and onion—then boil it till the bread is quite soft, beat it well, put in a quarter of a pound of butter, two spoonsful of thick cream, and put it in the dish with the turkey.

Stuffed Roast Turkey
(with Oyster Sauce or Bread Sauce)

SERVES 8

American turkeys were so plentiful that colonists ate them year-round instead of just on festive occasions. Introduced to Europe by the Spanish in the fifteenth century, turkeys became an English favorite early in the next century. Note: The sauces can be made just before serving, and kept warm on the stove.

For the Stuffing:
1 loaf white bread, shredded
¼ pound beef suet (may substitute 1 cup vegetable shortening)
½ pound sausage
¼ teaspoon nutmeg
½ teaspoon black pepper
1 teaspoon salt
2 eggs

For the Turkey:
1 (12-pound) turkey, thawed according to package directions

For the Oyster Sauce:
1 pint oysters, plus the liquor
2 tablespoons butter, melted
2 tablespoons flour
1 teaspoon Lemon Pickle (see page 155), may substitute zest of half a lemon
Salt and pepper, to taste

For the Bread Sauce:
2 slices white bread, crumbled
1 small onion, minced
¼ teaspoon ground cloves
¼ teaspoon nutmeg
¼ teaspoon pepper
½ teaspoon salt
4 tablespoons butter, melted
2 tablespoons cream

To make the Stuffing

Knead together the bread, suet, sausage, nutmeg, pepper, and salt. Beat the eggs and blend into this mixture.

To cook the Turkey

Wash it all over and discard the neck and giblets. Preheat oven to 325°F.

Fill the cavity with the stuffing. Close the opening and fasten the drumsticks to the tail with skewers or kitchen twine. Place the turkey breast side up on the rack in a roasting pan. Cover the turkey with a tent of aluminum foil, and roast for 3½ to 4½ hours, basting every 45 minutes. When turkey is one-third of the way done, remove the skewers/twine from the drumsticks. Remove the tent for the final 15 minutes of cooking time.

To make the Oyster Sauce

Bring 2 cups water to a boil in a saucepan, reduce the heat to low, add the oysters and their liquor, and simmer for 20 minutes. Strain the stock and reserve it. Set the oysters aside while you make the sauce.

Blend the butter and flour in a cup and add this, plus 1 cup of the oyster stock, to a saucepan over medium-low heat. Simmer, stirring constantly, until the sauce thickens. Stir in the oysters, Lemon Pickle, salt, and pepper. Simmer 5 minutes more.

To make the Bread Sauce

In a saucepan, bring 1 cup water to boil over high heat.

Add the bread crumbs, onion, and spices, and boil 15 minutes.

Remove from heat and stir in the butter and cream.

Serve the sauces on the side, and pass around the table.

FRICASSEE OF
SMALL CHICKENS.

TAKE off the legs and wings of four chickens, separate the breasts from the backs, cut off the necks and divide the backs across, clean the gizzards nicely, put them with the livers and other parts of the chicken, after being washed clean, into a sauce pan, add pepper, salt, and a little mace, cover them with water, and stew them till tender—then take them out, thicken half a pint of the water with two table spoonsful of flour rubbed into four ounces of butter, add half a pint of new milk, boil all together a few minutes, then add a gill of white wine, stirring it in carefully that it may not curdle; put the chickens in, and continue to shake the pan until they are sufficiently hot, and serve them up.

Chicken Fricassee
SERVES 4

Fricassee is a traditional French dish dating to the middle ages. A fricassee is a cooking process that usually combines sautéing, then adding liquids. Randolph's recipe is unusual in that she cooks the chicken in water before adding milk and wine.

1 (3-pound) chicken, cut in pieces (may also use the giblets)

1 teaspoon salt

½ teaspoon pepper

¼ teaspoon mace

8 tablespoons (1 stick) butter, melted

2 tablespoons flour

1 cup whole milk

½ cup white wine

Place the chicken pieces in Dutch oven with enough water to cover. Add the spices and bring to boil over medium-high heat. Reduce the heat to medium-low and simmer for 40 minutes.

Remove the chicken pieces and set them aside.

Discard all but 1 cup of the water left in the Dutch oven.

Combine the butter and flour to make a paste, and stir this into the water in the Dutch oven over medium heat. Add the milk and wine and stir until the sauce thickens. Pour over the chicken and serve immediately.

TO ROAST LARGE FOWLS.

TAKE the fowls when they are ready dressed, put them down to a good fire, dredge and baste them well with lard; they will be near an hour in roasting; make a gravy of the necks and gizzards, strain it, put in a spoonful of brown flour; when you dish them, pour on the gravy, and serve them up with egg sauce in a boat.

TO MAKE EGG SAUCE.

BOIL four eggs for ten minutes, chop half the whites, put them with the yelks, and chop them both together, but not very fine; put them into a quarter of a pound of good melted butter, and put it in a boat.

Roast Chicken in Egg Sauce

SERVES 4

Randolph's recipe calls for a simple egg sauce, distinct from Hollandaise, which would only use the egg yolks and add lemon juice.

1 (3½- to 4-pound) chicken

3 tablespoons butter, room temperature

1 teaspoon salt

½ teaspoon pepper

For the Egg Sauce:
4 hardboiled eggs

1 stick butter, melted

Preheat oven to 350°F.

Rub the outside of the chicken with butter; sprinkle all over with salt and pepper. Roast for 1½ hours until the meat is fork tender.

To make the Egg Sauce
Shell the eggs and cut them in half. Discard the whites of 2 eggs. Dice the 2 remaining whites and 4 egg yolks, and stir into a bowl with the melted butter. Serve warm.

TO ROAST WILD DUCKS OR TEAL.

WHEN the ducks are ready dressed, put in them a small onion, pepper, salt, and a spoonful of red wine; if the fire be good, they will roast in twenty minutes; make gravy of the necks and gizzards, a spoonful of red wine, half an anchovy, a blade or two of mace, one onion, and a little cayenne pepper; boil it till it is wasted to half a pint, strain it through a hair sieve, and pour it on the ducks—serve them up with onion sauce in a boat; garnish the dish with raspings of bread.

TO MAKE ONION SAUCE.

BOIL eight or ten large onions, change the water two or three times while they are boiling; when enough, chop them on a board to keep them a good colour, put them in a sauce pan with a quarter of a pound of butter and two spoonsful of thick cream; boil it a little, and pour it over the ducks.

Roast Wild Duck in Onion Sauce

SERVES 2-3

1 (5-pound) duck, cleaned and dressed

1 onion, peeled

¼ cup red wine

Salt and pepper, to taste

½ teaspoon anchovy paste

½ teaspoon mace

¼ teaspoon cayenne pepper

For the Onion Sauce:

4 large onions, finely chopped

4 tablespoons butter, melted

1 tablespoon whole milk, or cream

Preheat oven to 375°F.

Stuff the duck with the onion and wine. Rub the cavity with salt and pepper. Place in an uncovered roasting pan, and roast for 2 hours, basting often with the wine during cooking, until the meat is fork tender.

Remove and discard the onion before serving.

To make the Onion Sauce

Saute the onions in melted butter in a large skillet over medium heat for 3 to 5 minutes, until translucent. Add ½ cup water and the milk or cream, reduce the heat to low, and simmer 10 minutes, stirring frequently, until the sauce has thickened. Pour over the duck and serve.

TO DRESS DUCKS WITH JUICE OF ORANGES.

THE ducks being singed, picked, and drawn, mince the livers with a little scraped bacon, some butter, green onions, sweet herbs and parsley, seasoned with salt, pepper, and mushrooms; these being all minced together, put them into the bodies of the ducks, and roast them, covered with slices of bacon, and wrapped up in paper; then put a little gravy, the juice of an orange, a few shallots minced, into a stew pan, and shake in a little pepper; when the ducks are roasted, take off the bacon, dish them, and pour your sauce with the juice of oranges over them, and serve them up hot.

Duck with Mushrooms in Orange Sauce

SERVES 2-3

There are more than two hundred varieties of edible mushrooms that can still be found growing wild in Virginia. The most recognizable are chanterelles, morels, and oyster mushrooms.

1 (5-pound) duck, with giblets

Salt and pepper, to taste

¼ pound bacon slices

½ pound mushrooms

1 tablespoon butter, melted

1 teaspoon basil

1 tablespoon dried parsley flakes, or ½ cup minced fresh parsley

1 cup chicken stock

1 orange, juiced

3 shallots, diced

Preheat oven to 375°F.

Clean and dress the duck, removing the giblets and setting them aside. Rub the cavity with salt and pepper.

Mince the giblets, 1 slice of bacon, and the mushrooms. Place in a large bowl, and stir together with the butter, basil, and parsley. Stuff the duck with this mixture.

Tie or skewer it securely. Prick the skin around the thigh, back and breast to allow fat to escape. Place in a roasting pan and cover the duck with the remaining slices of bacon.

In a bowl, stir together the chicken stock, orange juice, and the shallots, and pour around the duck. Roast for 2 hours, until the meat is fork tender. Transfer the duck to shallow-sided serving dish. Skim, then strain the liquid left in the roasting pan, and pour over the duck before serving.

TO MAKE A DISH OF CURRY AFTER THE EAST INDIAN MANNER.

CUT two chickens as for fricassee, wash them clean, and put them in a stew pan with as much water as will cover them; sprinkle them with a large spoonful of salt, and let them boil till tender, covered close all the time, and skim them well; when boiled enough, take up the chickens, and put the liquor of them into a pan, then put half a pound of fresh butter in the pan, and brown it a little; put into it two cloves of garlic, and a large onion sliced, and let these all fry till brown, often shaking the pan; then put in the chickens, and sprinkle over them two or three spoonsful of curry powder; then cover the pan close, and let the chickens do till brown, often shaking the pan; then put in the liquor the chickens were boiled in, and let all stew till tender; if acid is agreeable squeeze the juice of a lemon or orange in it.

Curried Chicken

SERVES 4

Randolph's curried chicken recipe is distinct from the famous Southern chicken curry dish, Country Captain. This version does not call for tomatoes and almonds.

1 (3-pound) chicken, cut in pieces

2 teaspoons salt

1 small onion, thinly sliced

1 clove garlic, crushed

4 tablespoons butter

1½ tablespoons Randolph's Spice Blend (see page 160), or curry powder

1 tablespoon lemon juice

2 tablespoons orange juice

Place the chicken pieces in a Dutch oven with enough water to cover. Add the salt, cover, and bring to a boil over medium-high heat, then reduce the heat to medium-low and simmer for 40 minutes.

In a skillet over medium heat, brown the onion and garlic in butter for 3 to 5 minutes, until the onions are translucent. Add these to the Dutch oven, along with the Spice Blend. Simmer for 15 minutes, then stir in the lemon and orange juice.

This recipe does well served over rice.

ROPA VEIJA—SPANISH.

PEEL the skin from ripe tomatos, put them in a pan with a spoonful of melted butter, some pepper and salt, shred cold meat or fowl; put it in, and fry it sufficiently.

Ropa Vieja

SERVES 6

Ropa Vieja, *or "old clothes" in Spanish, is a dish that originates in the Canary Islands and was brought to the Caribbean, where it became the national dish of Cuba. If using beef, slow-cooked roast works well.*

1 tablespoon butter

10–12 small tomatoes, peeled, or 1 (32-ounce) can

2 pounds beef or chicken, cooked and shredded

1 teaspoon salt

⅛ teaspoon pepper

Melt the butter in a sauté pan over medium heat and add the shredded meat, salt, and pepper. Reduce the heat to medium-low and simmer for 45 minutes, or until the tomatoes have cooked down. Serve hot.

TO MAKE CROQUETS.

TAKE cold fowl or fresh meat of any kind, with slices of ham, fat and lean—chop them together very fine, add half as much stale bread grated, salt, pepper, grated nutmeg, a tea-spoonful of made mustard, a table-spoonful of catsup, and a lump of butter; knead all well together till it resembles sausage meat, make them in cakes, dip them in the yelk of an egg beaten, cover them thickly with grated bread, and fry them a light brown.

Croquettes

MAKES 24 CROQUETTES, SERVES 8

Croquettes appeared at Versailles, the court of French King Louis XIV, at the end of the seventeenth century. Those used a filling of sweetbreads, cheese, and truffles. More commonly, it became a way to use leftover stewed meats.

½ cup butter, divided

1 cup white bread, cubed

3 cups ground meat (chicken, turkey, beef, or lamb)

1½ teaspoons salt

½ teaspoon pepper

¼ teaspoon nutmeg

1 teaspoon store-bought yellow mustard

1 tablespoon Mushroom Catsup (see page 156), may substitute Worcestershire sauce

3 egg yolks, beaten

1½ cups fine bread crumbs

Melt ¼ cup butter and stir it into the bread cubes in a large bowl. Add the meat, salt, pepper, nutmeg, mustard, and Mushroom Catsup and blend well. Shape into croquettes.

Brush with the egg yolk and roll them in the dry bread crumbs.

Melt the remaining butter in a large skillet over medium-high heat, and cook the croquettes for 3 to 4 minutes, turning so they brown on all sides and are cooked through.

MACCARONI PUDDING.

SIMMER half a pound of maccaroni in a plenty of water, with a table-spoonful of salt, till tender, but not broke—strain it, beat five yelks, two whites of eggs, half a pint of cream—mince white meat and boiled ham very fine, add three spoonsful of grated cheese, pepper and salt; mix these with the maccaroni, butter the mould, put it in, and steam it in a pan of boiling water for an hour—serve with rich gravy.

Macaroni Casserole

SERVES 6

In good English cooking tradition, this "pudding" is cooked by steaming, rather like we would cook a custard. However, the modern version simply calls for baking. It is a great way to use leftover chicken and ham.

1 (8-ounce) package macaroni

1 cup grated sharp cheddar cheese

½ cup cream

1 cup bread crumbs

3 eggs, beaten

½ teaspoon salt

Dash pepper

6 ounces cooked chicken, cut in ½-inch cubes

6 ounces cooked ham, cut in ½-inch cubes

Cook the macaroni according to package directions.

Preheat oven to 350°F.

Stir together all ingredients and pour into a greased casserole. Bake for 40 to 45 minutes, just until it begins to brown. Serve hot.

EGGS A-LA-CREME.

BOIL twelve eggs just hard enough to allow you to cut them in slices—cut some crusts of bread very thin, put them in the bottom and round the sides of a moderately deep dish, place the eggs in, strewing each layer with the stale bread grated, and some pepper and salt.

SAUCE A-LA-CREME, FOR THE EGGS.

PUT a quarter of a pound of butter, with a large table-spoonful of flour rubbed well into it in a sauce pan; add some chopped parsley, a little onion, salt, pepper, nutmeg, and a gill of cream; stir it over the fire until it begins to boil, then pour it over the eggs, cover the top with grated bread, set it in a Dutch oven with a heated top, and when a light brown, send it to table.

Eggs à la Crème

SERVES 6

Different from the famous scrambled egg dish of the same name that is frequently served in Cajun country, Randolph's recipe is more of an egg casserole. It is ideal for serving at brunch.

2 cups grated bread crumbs, divided into 3 portions

Salt and pepper, to taste

12 soft-boiled eggs, sliced

For the Sauce:
8 tablespoons (1 stick) butter, melted

1 tablespoon flour

1 tablespoon dried parsley flakes, or ½ cup minced fresh parsley

1 tablespoon onion, minced

½ teaspoon salt

¼ teaspoon pepper

¼ teaspoon nutmeg

4 ounces cream

Preheat oven to 350°F.

Cover the bottom of a baking dish with bread crumbs. Salt and pepper lightly. Layer a portion of the eggs atop the bread crumbs. Continue layering, ending with the bread crumbs on top. Cover with the sauce (see below) and bake 20 minutes, or until golden brown.

To make the Sauce

In a small saucepan over medium heat, blend together the butter and flour. Add the parsley, onion, salt, pepper, and nutmeg. Stir in the cream, and simmer for 5 minutes until the sauce thickens.

EGGS AND TOMATOS.

PEEL the skins from a dozen large tomatos, put four ounces of butter in a frying pan, add some salt, pepper, and a little chopped onion; fry them a few minutes, add the tomatos, and chop them while frying; when nearly done, break in six eggs, stir them quickly, and serve them up.

Scrambled Eggs with Tomatoes

SERVES 4

The tomato, native to central Mexico, quickly gained acceptance in Southern Europe when it was introduced by the Spanish in the fifteenth and early sixteenth centuries. However, it was slow to gain popularity in Britain, where people believed tomatoes to be poisonous. This may be because the acid in the tomato leached lead out of the pewter plates that were used at the time.

4 tablespoons butter

½ cup onion, chopped

½ teaspoon salt

¼ teaspoon pepper

6 tomatoes, peeled and diced

3 eggs, beaten

In a frying pan over medium heat, melt the butter and sauté the onion for 3 to 5 minutes, until translucent. Add the salt and pepper, stir in the tomatoes, and continue to cook for 5 minutes. Stir in the eggs and cook, stirring occasionally, until done to your liking.

COOKERY BOOKS AND CULINARY TRADITIONS IN
The Virginia Housewife

In writing her cookbook, Mary Randolph followed a fine tradition of women authors dating to the late sixteenth century. Unlike in France where male chefs authored works for a predominantly male audience, in Britain women wrote for women, although some of the earliest authors used male pseudonyms. In the first half of the seventeenth century they began publishing under their own names, but were discreet, using their initials, trade cards, or phrases such as "By a Lady."[1] After 1750, female authors began to take credit for their work and used their reputations as cooks or housekeepers to sell their books. But these were largely servants, unlike earlier authors who had been women of higher social standing. With the rise of the consumer revolution and the growth of literacy in Britain, increasing numbers of women from lower classes bought cookery books. Some 425 new ones were published in Britain in the seventeenth century. With reprints, this means an estimated 531,250 volumes were produced.[2]

Not surprisingly, British cookbook authors dominated the trade in the American colonies. The first cookbook printed in America appeared in Williamsburg, Virginia, in 1742. It was an edition of Mrs. E. Smith's *The Compleat Housewife; or, Accomplished Gentlewoman's Companion*, first published in 1727. When William Parks, the editor of the *Virginia Gazette*, printed the work, it was in its tenth edition in Britain, although he based his version on the fifth edition of 1732. It was not a complete copy of Smith's book. Parks explained in the preface of his version that he left out "Recipes, the Ingredients or Materials for which, are not to be had in the Country."[3]

But Parks was being disingenuous; the ingredients included in the recipes he omitted were plentiful in Virginia. He cut particular recipes because they did not appeal to him personally and he felt their inclusion would "swell out the Book and increase its Price."[4] The book sold well and Parks' successor William Hunter reprinted it in 1752. It was the only serious attempt to market an American-produced cookbook for fifty years.[5]

The first cookbook credited to an American author was also by a woman. Amelia Simmons published *American Cookery, or The Art of Dressing Viands, Fish, Poultry and Vegetables, and the Best Modes of Making Pastes, Puffs, Pies, Tarts, Puddings, Custards and Preserves, and All Kinds of Cakes . . . Adapted to This Country, and All Grades of Life* in Hartford, Connecticut in 1796. She lifted many of the recipes directly from English author Susannah

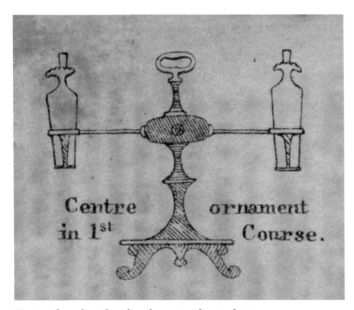

During the colonial and early national periods, it was common to use serving pieces such as epergnes or cruet stands such as this one as centerpieces. The Virginia House-Wife, *2nd ed., p. 256, insert 3, detail. Henry Stone, lithographer.*

Carter's 1772 cookbook, *The Frugal Housewife*, but she added several original recipes that included indigenous American foods, including cornmeal, cranberries, and turkey. Though Simmons's work lacked originality—it was essentially English—it was nonetheless quite popular. A dozen reprints and pirated editions appeared before 1830. An American edition of Susannah Carter's book came out in 1803 with an appendix of recipes "adapted to the American mode of cookery."[6] A printer in Alexandria, Virginia, used the identical section in a reprint of English author Hannah Glasse's 1747 classic *Art of Cookery Made Plain and Easy* in 1805. But of the twenty-six additional recipes, only eighteen of them had American origins. And the appendix may have been lifted from an almanac.[7] For fifty years after the publication of Amelia Simmons's book, no significant cookbook by an American author appeared until *The Virginia Housewife*.[8]

Collecting recipes and advice on household management was a common activity among members of Virginia's gentry. In the seventeenth century, women carefully recorded recipes they created, learned from others, or found in published works, binding the manuscript pages into book form. Mothers often organized and copied their collections into blank books to share with their daughters. Frequently, they presented them to their daughters when they married and left to set up their own homes. Martha Washington inherited such a manuscript from her first mother-in-law Frances Parke Custis. The pages contained recipes dating to the late seventeenth century, probably copied from an earlier manuscript, and Martha added to these for the next five decades before she in her turn passed the book on to her granddaughter Nelly Parke Custis Lewis.[9] At least two such manuscript collections of recipes had passed through the Randolph family, one dating from around 1700, and the other—the collection of Jane Bolling Randolph—from 1743. In recording her recipes, Mary Randolph

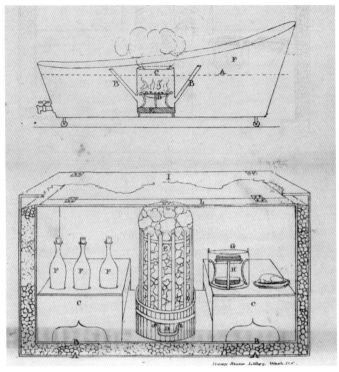

Randolph included illustrations and descriptions for inventions such as a water heater and refrigerator in the second edition of The Virginia House-Wife *(1825), p. 256, insert 3, detail. Henry Stone, lithographer.*

was following in a long and venerable tradition.[10]

Randolph assembled her cookbook out of years of extensive personal experience. In the preface to *The Virginia Housewife*, she explained, "The greater part of the following receipts have been written from memory, where they were impressed by long continued practice."[11] She may have produced the work in part because she had no daughters with whom to share her vast knowledge. Indeed, in the closing pages of the book, she added practical household advice such as how to manufacture vinegars useful as air fresheners, soap, starch, blacking, and candles, as well as how to polish silver and clean cutlery for homemakers.[12] But it was her food that was at the

heart of Randolph's book. She hoped that her recipes would appeal to a wide audience, writing, "Should they prove serviceable to the young inexperienced housekeeper, it will add greatly to that gratification which an extensive circulation of the work will like to confer."[13] Her work exceeded all expectations and sold to experienced cooks as well as young wives. When putting together her own personal recipe collection, Martha Jefferson Randolph carefully copied out more than fifty recipes from *The Virginia Housewife*, crediting her sister-in-law before passing the manuscript on to her daughter Virginia Jefferson Randolph Trist in classic Southern fashion.[14]

Randolph's cookbook was both modern and practical. She explained in her preface, "The difficulties I encountered when I first entered on the duties of a House-keeping life, from the want of books sufficiently clear and concise, to impart knowledge to a Tyro, compelled me to study the subject, and by actual experiment, to reduce every thing, in the culinary line, to proper weights and measures."[15] To appeal to tyros or neophytes, she wrote in an extremely readable style. She did not include incredibly elaborate dishes that appeared frequently in English cookbooks but were used in very few households. Similarly, she advised her readers not to overwhelm their guests with a vast array dishes during a meal:

> *Profusion is not elegance—a dinner justly calculated for the company, and consisting for the greater part of small articles, correctly prepared, and neatly served up, will make a much more pleasing appearance to the sight, and give a far greater gratification to the appetite, than a table loaded with food, and from the multiplicity of dishes, unavoidably neglected in the preparation and served up cold.*[16]

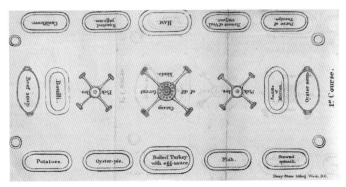

Among other illustrations in the second edition, Randolph provided suggested table settings. "1st Course," The Virginia House-Wife, 2nd ed., p. 256, insert 1. Henry Stone, lithographer.

One thing of which Randolph did approve was using plenty of vegetables. More than forty different varieties of vegetables appear in her recipes.[17] This reflected a major change occurring in American diets beginning around 1780 as vegetable consumption increased dramatically. Cooks began preparing individual vegetable dishes instead of just boiling items together in stews and other one-pot meals. This trend began among the wealthy, but quickly spread to members of all classes in America.[18] In her recipes, Randolph repeatedly stressed that vegetables be cooked sparingly to crispness, a far cry from the stewed vegetables that later became prevalent in Southern cooking.[19] In preparing asparagus, for example, she admonished, "Great care must be taken to watch the exact time of their becoming tender; take them just at that instant, and they will have their true flavor and colour; a minute or two more boiling destroys both."[20] Similarly, for greens such as spinach, "a few minutes will boil it sufficiently."[21] If at all possible, Randolph preferred to serve fresh vegetables. Discussing peas, she stressed, "To have them in perfection, they must be quite young, gathered early in the morning, kept in a cool place and

not shelled until they are to be dressed. . . ."[22] As for eggplant, "The purple ones are best, get them young and fresh. . . ."[23] Despite such admonitions for freshness, Randolph's work also reflected a second trend that developed in the American diet at the end of the seventeenth century, i.e., using stores of preserved foods—meats, vegetables, ciders, etc.—instead of relying only on ingredients available at certain seasons of the year.[24] The pages of *The Virginia Housewife* are filled with recipes for preserving ingredients for future use.

Widely acknowledged as the first collection of Southern recipes, *The Virginia Housewife* reflects a cuisine with a wide range of cultural influences, variety, and sophistication. Unsurprisingly, it is based primarily on English cooking traditions, but even so, by including seventeen different herbs and additional seasonings in her recipes, Randolph altered British dishes to Southern tastes. Adding "a few cloves of garlic" in her Scotch Collops of Veal, for example, reveals that the Virginia palate preferred more intense flavors than its British or Northern counterparts.[25] Native American influences can be found among the recipes through the use of American vegetables and grains such as squash and corn, as well as techniques for barbequing meats, particularly shoat or young pig. African and Caribbean traditions contributed by enslaved black women appeared in the pages through foods such as rice, sorghum, and bananas, as well as dishes like gumbo. The presence of French Huguenots in seventeenth-century Virginia, refugees of the French Revolution, and the influence of Randolph's cousin, Francophile Thomas Jefferson, meant that French fare was present as well, represented by breads, fritters, french fries (i.e. To Fry Sliced Potatoes), and more than a dozen flavors of ice cream. Spanish dishes such as To Make an Ollo—A Spanish Dish, Ropa Veija—Spanish, and Gaspacio—Spanish appear either because of the close proximity of Spanish America or through the agency of Randolph's sister, Harriet Randolph Hackley, who lived for a while in Cadiz, Spain.[26] *The Virginia Housewife* includes recipes for Italian polenta and pastas. Randolph even introduced Americans to macaroni and cheese.[27] Possibly the most surprising foreign influence in the book is South Asian, evidenced in Randolph's recipe for curry powder.

Scalloped Tomatoes

Chapter 3

VEGETABLES, PICKLING, ETC.

VEGETABLES.

TO DRESS SALAD.

TO have this delicate dish in perfection, the lettuce, pepper grass, chervil, cress, etc. should be gathered early in the morning, nicely picked, washed, and laid in cold water, which will be improved by adding ice; just before dinner is ready to be served, drain the water from your salad, cut it into a bowl, giving the proper proportions of each plant; prepare the following mixture to pour over it: boil two fresh eggs ten minutes, put them in water to cool, then take the yelks in a soup plate, pour on them a table spoonful of cold water, rub them with a wooden spoon until they are perfectly dissolved; then add two spoonsful of oil: when well mixed, put in a tea-spoonful of salt, one of powdered sugar, and one of made mustard; when all these are united and quite smooth, stir in two table spoonsful of common, and two of tarragon vinegar; put it over the salad, and garnish the top with the whites of the eggs cut into rings, and lay around the edge of the bowl young scallions, they being the most delicate of the onion tribe.

Garden Salad with Tarragon Dressing

SERVES 6

Garden salads have been served since ancient times, although green salads did not become popular in Britain until the seventeenth century, after the tradition was reintroduced from the continent. In his 1727 work, The Practical Kitchen Gardener, *naturalist Stephen Switzer noted some thirty or so different varieties of greens, many of which were introduced to England from Italy.*

24 ounces mixed salad greens

2 hardboiled eggs, sliced in rounds, yolks removed and saved

2 tablespoons oil

1 teaspoon powdered sugar

1 teaspoon store-bought yellow mustard

2 tablespoons white vinegar

2 tablespoons tarragon vinegar

1 bunch young scallions, or green onions, whole or chopped

1 teaspoon salt

Wash and dry the salad greens, and place in a serving bowl.

In a separate bowl, add water to the yolks and stir into a paste. Whisk in the oil, salt, sugar, mustard, and vinegars, and dress the salad.

Garnish with the circles of egg white and the scallions, either whole or chopped.

POTATOS MASHED
WITH ONIONS.

PREPARE some onions by putting them through a sieve, and mix them with potatos; in proportioning the onions to the potatos, you will be guided by your wish to have more or less of their flavour.

Onion Mashed Potatoes

SERVES 6

Potatoes are another New World food introduced to Europe by the Spanish in the sixteenth century, although it took another century before the British developed mashed potatoes.

4 medium potatoes, peeled and cubed

4 tablespoons butter, divided

1 medium onion, finely chopped

½ cup, or more, whole milk

Salt and pepper, to taste

Place the potato cubes in a pot of boiling water and cook about 15 minutes, or until tender.

In a separate pan over medium heat, melt 2 tablespoons butter and sauté the onions 3 to 5 minutes, until translucent. Set aside.

Drain and mash the potatoes, adding the remaining butter and enough milk to obtain your desired consistency. Add the onions, salt and pepper to taste, and any additional milk as needed, and whip until creamy. Serve hot.

POTATO BALLS.

MIX mashed potatos with the yelk of an egg, roll them into balls, flour them, or cover them with egg and bread crumbs, fry them in clean dripping, or brown them in a Dutch oven. They are an agreeable vegetable relish, and a supper dish.

Potato Balls

A wonderful recipe using leftover mashed potatoes, this recipe works just as well with onion mashed potatoes. They can be either fried or baked.

1½ cups cold mashed potatoes

1 egg, separated

½ cup flour, or ½ cup fine bread crumbs

Cooking oil for frying

Mix the potatoes with the egg yolk in a bowl. Roll into 1- or 2-inch balls.

Place the flour or bread crumbs in a shallow bowl or plate, and roll the balls in flour to coat.

In a heavy skillet, heat 2 inches of oil to 375°F. Fry the balls in oil, turning, until golden brown. Do not crowd the pan.

Alternatively, Preheat oven to 350°F.

Line a baking sheet with parchment paper.

Dip the prepared potato balls in the egg white, and roll in the bread crumbs.

Place the balls on the parchment-lined baking sheet and bake 15 to 20 minutes, or until brown.

TO SCOLLOP TOMATOS.

PEEL off the skin from large, full, ripe tomatos—put a layer in the bottom of a deep dish, cover it well with bread grated fine; sprinkle on pepper and salt, and lay some bits of butter over them—put another layer of each, till the dish is full— let the top be covered with crumbs and butter—bake it a nice brown.

Scalloped Tomatoes

SERVES 6

The origin of the cooking term scalloped *is obscure, but likely means "breaded."*

2 pounds tomatoes, peeled and diced, or 1 (28-ounce) can diced tomatoes, drained

1½ cups fine bread crumbs

Salt and pepper, to taste

¼ cup butter, melted

Preheat oven to 375°F.

Arrange half the tomatoes in a layer on the bottom of a casserole dish or oven-safe skillet.

Sprinkle half of the bread crumbs over the tomatoes. Salt and pepper according to taste. Sprinkle with half the butter.

Repeat the process, ending with butter.

Bake for 20 minutes, or until the crumbs are brown.

PUREE OF TURNIPS.

PARE a dozen large turnips, slice them, and put them into a stew-pan, with four ounces of butter and a little salt; set the pan over a moderate fire, turn them often with a wooden spoon; when they look white, add a ladle full of veal gravy, stew them till it becomes thick; skim it, and pass it through a sieve; put the turnips in a dish, and pour the gravy over them.

Whipped Turnips with Brown Gravy

SERVES 6

Turnips are less starchy than potatoes when whipped, and they have a sharper flavor.

2 pounds turnips, peeled and cubed

½ teaspoon salt

½ cup butter

For the Brown Gravy:

4 tablespoons butter, melted

¼ cup flour

½ teaspoon salt

¼ teaspoon pepper

2 cups beef broth

1 teaspoon Kitchen Bouquet (optional)

Add the turnips and salt to a pot with enough water to cover, and bring to a boil over medium-high heat. Boil 20 minutes, or until the turnips are soft.

Drain the turnips, add the butter, and mash. Serve with Brown Gravy.

To make the Brown Gravy

In a saucepan, stir together the butter, flour, salt, and pepper. Add the broth and the Kitchen Bouquet if desired and continue to stir over medium heat until the gravy thickens.

RAGOUT OF TURNIPS.

PEEL as many small turnips as will fill a dish; put them into a stew pan with some butter and a little sugar, set them over a hot stove, shake them about, and turn them till they are a good brown; pour in half a pint of rich high seasoned gravy; stew the turnips till tender, and serve them with the gravy poured over them.

Turnip Ragout

SERVES 4

In Europe, turnips grow extremely large and can weigh in at more than two pounds. In Ireland, they were used to carve the original jack-o-lanterns.

2 pounds small turnips, washed, pared, and cut in 1-inch cubes

3 tablespoons butter

1½ teaspoons sugar

1 cup beef broth

Salt to taste

Place the turnips in a saucepan with enough water to cover, bring to a boil over medium-high heat, and continue to boil for 5 minutes. Allow to cool slightly, then drain.

Melt the butter in a separate large saucepan over medium-low heat and stir in the sugar. Add the turnips and stir for 5 minutes to caramelize, or until they begin to brown. Stir in the broth and increase the heat to medium-high. Bring to a boil, then reduce the heat to medium and simmer, covered, for 10 minutes or until the turnips are tender. Serve with Brown Gravy (see page 141).

EGG PLANT.

THE purple ones are best; get them young and fresh; pull out the stem, and parboil them to take off the bitter taste; cut them in slices an inch thick, but do not peel them; dip them in the yelk of an egg, and cover them with grated bread, a little salt and pepper—when this has dried, cover the other side the same way—fry them a nice brown. They are very delicious, tasting much like soft crabs. The egg plant may be dressed in another manner: scrape the rind and parboil them; cut a slit from one end to the other, take out the seeds, fill the space with a rich forcemeat, and stew them in well seasoned gravy, or bake them, and serve up with gravy in the dish.

Stuffed Eggplant

Fried Eggplant

SERVES 2

Eggplant, or aubergine *as it is known in Britain, is actually a berry, although it is usually thought to be a vegetable. It originated in India, was taken to Britain by the sixteenth century, and from there introduced to America. The name "eggplant" appeared by 1763, and derives from white varietals that are indeed egg-shaped.*

1 small eggplant

1 egg yolk

½ teaspoon salt

¼ teaspoon pepper

1 cup bread crumbs

1 tablespoon oil or butter

Wash, pare, and slice the eggplant into ¼-inch-thick slices.

In a bowl, mix the egg yolk with 1 tablespoon water, the salt, and pepper.

Place the bread crumbs in a separate shallow bowl or plate.

Dip the eggplant slices into the egg mixture and roll in crumbs. Let stand 5 minutes to dry.

Heat the oil or butter in a skillet over medium-high heat and fry the eggplant slowly until both sides are crisp and brown. Transfer to a paper towel to drain. Serve hot.

Stuffed Eggplant

SERVES 4

1 large eggplant

1 pound Forcemeat (see page 59), may substitute mild pork sausage

Preheat oven to 350°F.

Slice the eggplant in half horizontally and scoop out the seeds.

Fill the cavity with Forcemeat.

Spray a baking dish with cooking spray and place both halves of the eggplant in it and bake for 50 minutes. Drain off the fat before serving.

SWEET POTATOS STEWED.

WASH and wipe them, and if they be large, cut them in two lengths; put them at the bottom of a stew pan, lay over some slices of boiled ham; and on that, one or two chickens cut up with pepper, salt, and a bundle of herbs; pour in some water, and stew them till done, then take out the herbs, serve the stew in a deep dish—thicken the gravy, and pour over it.

Stewed Sweet Potatoes and Chicken

SERVES 6-8

Although the terms sweet potato *and* yam *are often used synonymously, they are in fact different root vegetables. The yam is related to the yucca family, has a whiter flesh, and is not as flavorful as the sweet potato.*

2 large sweet potatoes, peeled

¼ pound ham, sliced

1 (3-pound) chicken, cut into pieces

1 tablespoon dried parsley flakes or 2 tablespoons minced fresh parsley

1 teaspoon sage

2 teaspoons salt

1 teaspoon pepper

2 cups water or chicken broth

Slice the sweet potatoes in half, lay them in the bottom of a Dutch oven, and cover with sliced ham. Add the chicken pieces, herbs, the spices, and water or chicken broth and bring to boil over high heat, then reduce the heat to medium-low and simmer 1 hour, adding more liquid as necessary to cover ingredients.

Allow the stew to cool enough to bone the chicken and discard the bones. If the broth needs thickening, mix 1 tablespoon flour and a little of the broth into a paste, and stir this into the stew to thicken.

FIELD PEAS.

THERE are many varieties of these peas; the smaller kind are the most delicate. Have them young and newly gathered, shell and boil them tender; pour them in a colander to drain; put some lard in a frying pan; when it boils, mash the peas, and fry them in a cake of a light brown; put it in the dish with the crust uppermost—garnish with thin bits of fried bacon. They are very nice when fried whole, so that each pea is distinct from the other; but they must be boiled less, and fried with great care. Plain boiling is a very common way of dressing them.

Black-Eyed Pea Cakes

SERVES 6

As Randolph points out in her introduction, there are many different types of field peas, but the one most associated with Southern cooking is the black-eyed pea. Originating in West Africa, the black-eyed pea arrived in Virginia in the seventeenth century and quickly spread throughout the South. It remains a staple in African-American and Southern food culture.

1 (15-ounce) can black-eyed peas, or ½ cup dried peas, soaked overnight in water and cooked according to package directions

1 tablespoon butter

2 slices bacon, cooked and minced

Drain and mash the black-eyed peas and form them into 12 to 15 (2½-inch-diameter) cakes.

Melt the butter in a skillet over medium-high heat and fry the cakes about 2 minutes per side until lightly brown. Garnish with bacon bits.

GASPACHO— SPANISH

PUT some soft biscuit or toasted bread in the bottom of a sallad bowl, put in a layer of sliced tomatos with the skin taken off, and one of sliced cucumbers, sprinkled with pepper, salt, and chopped onion; do this until the bowl is full; stew some tomatos quite soft, strain the juice, mix in some mustard, oil, and water, and pour over it; make it two hours before it is eaten.

Gazpacho

SERVES 8

Traditionally, Gazpacho is a cold soup made of chopped tomatoes and cucumbers that developed in the region of Andalusia in Southern Spain. Randolph's version is more of a marinated vegetable salad—also perfect for summer dining.

1 cup bread crumbs, divided

3 pounds tomatoes, skinned and sliced

2 cucumbers, peeled and thinly sliced

Salt and pepper, to taste

1 onion, diced

3 cups tomato juice

¼ cup wine vinegar

½ cup cooking oil

1 tablespoon store-bought yellow mustard

Line the bottom of a medium serving bowl with a portion of the bread crumbs. Arrange a layer of tomatoes on top of the bread crumbs, then a layer of cucumbers. Lightly salt and pepper, then sprinkle with layer of onions. Repeat the layers until the bowl is filled.

Whisk together the tomato juice, vinegar, oil, and mustard. Pour over the gazpacho, cover, and refrigerate for 2 hours before serving.

CABBAGE A-LA-CREME.

TAKE two good heads of cabbage, cut out the stalks, boil it tender, with a little salt in the water—have ready one large spoonful of butter, and a small one of flour rubbed into it, half a pint of milk, with pepper and salt; make it hot, put the cabbage in after pressing out the water, and stew it till quite tender.

Cabbage à la Crème

SERVES 8

Cabbage à la Crème is a terrific vegetable for traditional meals, but it is also great for summer picnics because it can be cooked on the grill, making a fine addition to other grilled vegetables like corn.

1 cabbage

2 teaspoons salt, divided

4 tablespoons butter, melted

2 tablespoons flour

½ cup whole milk

½ teaspoon pepper

Wash and core the cabbage and remove the outer leaves. Cut the cabbage into wedges or ½-inch slices.

In a large pot, add 1 teaspoon salt to 5 cups water and bring to boil over medium-high heat. Add the cabbage to the pot and boil 10 to 15 minutes, until tender. Drain and set aside.

Blend the butter and flour in the pot. Stir in the milk, 1 teaspoon salt, and the pepper. Add the cabbage back to the pot and simmer over medium-low heat until warmed.

To make individual servings, baked or grilled
1 (10-inch) square piece aluminum foil

1 cup chopped cabbage

1 tablespoon cream

1–2 tablespoons butter

Salt and pepper, to taste

Stir all ingredients together in a small bowl and place on a 10-inch square of aluminum foil. Brings sides together and fold over or pinch to seal. Bake at 400°F for 25 to 30 minutes, or cook on a grill.

MACARONI.

BOIL as much macaroni as will fill your dish, in milk and water, till quite tender; drain it on a sieve sprinkle a little salt over it, put a layer in your dish then cheese and butter as in the polenta, and bake it in the same manner.

Macaroni and Cheese

SERVES 6

Although simple, this is the first recipe for macaroni and cheese published in America. Randolph may have learned the recipe through her cousin Thomas Jefferson, whose enslaved chef James Hemings (brother of Sally) learned to make the dish while living in Paris. Jefferson loved the dish, bought a macaroni machine, and imported macaroni from Europe. While president, he served the dish at one of the first state dinners at the White House in 1802.

8 ounces macaroni

2 cups sharp cheddar cheese, cut in ½-inch cubes, or 1½ cups grated, plus more for topping

1¼ cups whole milk

½ teaspoon salt

Cook the macaroni according to package directions, and drain.

Preheat oven to 350°F.

Combine the remaining ingredients in a large bowl. Stir in the macaroni. Pour into a greased casserole and bake for 45 minutes. For the last 15 minutes of baking time, you may add additional cheese and/or buttered bread crumbs to the top and brown.

PICKLING, ETC.

 ## LEMON PICKLE.

GRATE the yellow rind from two dozen fine fresh lemons, quarter them but leave them whole at the bottom; sprinkle salt on them, and put them in the sun every day until dry; then brush off the salt, put them in a pot with one ounce of nutmegs, and one of mace pounded; a large handful of horse radish scraped and dried two dozen cloves of garlic, and a pint of mustard seed; pour on one gallon of strong vinegar, tie the pot close, put a board on, and let it stand three months—strain it, and when perfectly clear, bottle it.

Lemon Pickle

MAKES ABOUT 2 QUARTS

Pickling has been used since ancient times as a way to preserve foodstuffs, either to eat separately or as ingredients in other recipes. The Virginia Housewife *uses Lemon Pickle in fourteen different recipes. Although it will have less of a sharp vinegar taste, fresh grated lemon peel makes for a good substitute.*

12 lemons

Salt

2 teaspoons nutmeg

1 teaspoon mace

¼ cup mustard seed

¼ cup horseradish

12 cloves garlic

2 quarts vinegar

Remove a very thin portion of peel from the lemons. Quarter them without cutting through the bottom. Sprinkle overall with salt and leave them in a warm place to dry.

When dry, brush the salt from the lemons and place them in a stone crock along with the nutmeg, mace, mustard seed, horseradish, and garlic.

Pour the vinegar over the other ingredients.

Cover the crock tightly and let it stand for 3 months in a cool dark place. Strain until clear and then bottle.

MUSHROOM CATSUP.

TAKE the flaps of the proper mushrooms from the stems—wash them, add some salt, and crush them; then boil them some time, strain them through a cloth, put them on the fire again with salt to your taste, a few cloves of garlic, and a quarter of an ounce of cloves pounded, to a peck of mushrooms; boil it till reduced to less than half the original quantity— bottle and cork it well.

Mushroom Catsup

YIELDS 1 PINT

Catsup is a table sauce developed in China in the seventeenth century. The British encountered it in the Malay Peninsula and it became extremely popular. Catsup can be made from a number of items—originally it was fish in brine—but the British primarily used mushrooms. Tomato catsup did not appear until the nineteenth century. Mushroom catsup was the go-to condiment in cooking during the Victorian era and is still commercially available in Britain.

2 pounds mushrooms

2 tablespoons salt

3 cloves garlic, crushed

1 teaspoon ground cloves

½ cup cider vinegar

Trim the stem ends from the mushrooms and discard. Slice the mushrooms. In a large covered pot, spread a layer of mushrooms on the bottom and sprinkle with salt. Continue to layer. Cover and let sit overnight.

After 24 hours, crush the mushrooms.

Add all remaining ingredients to the mushrooms and bring to boil over medium-high heat.

Reduce heat to medium-low and simmer for 10 minutes.

Strain through a sieve, pressing to remove all liquid, and discard the mushroom pieces.

Pour the liquid into a sterile jar and seal with a lid.

Can keep in a dark, cool place for 3 months before using. Will keep for about 1 year once open.

TO MAKE WALNUT CATSUP.

GATHER the walnuts as for pickling, and keep them in salt and water the same time; then pound them in a marble mortar—to every dozen walnuts, put a quart of vinegar; stir them well every day for a week, then put them in a bag, and press all the liquor through; to each quart, put a tea-spoonful of pounded cloves, and one of mace, with six cloves of garlic—boil it fifteen or twenty minutes, and bottle it.

Walnut Catsup

MAKES 1 QUART

Unlike its cousin Mushroom Catsup, Walnut Catsup is no longer manufactured commercially. Although it is a vinegar and not nearly as viscus, its flavor is almost identical to A-1 Steak Sauce.

12 walnuts

5 tablespoons salt

1 quart vinegar

1 teaspoon ground cloves

1 teaspoon mace

6 cloves garlic, crushed

In a large pot, bring 2 quarts of water to boil. Scald the nuts for 5 minutes, then let cool before removing the green outer shells.

Add the nuts to a large lidded container, and cover the walnuts quickly with a solution of the salt and 1 quart of water. Leave for 9 days, covered, changing the solution twice

After 9 days, wear rubber gloves to avoid being stained, and drain and wipe the nuts.

Pound them with a mortar. Put the pieces in a jar and pour in the vinegar. Let stand for 1 week, stirring daily, then strain the liquid into a pot. Press the nuts to capture all the juice, then discard the solids. Add the cloves, mace, and garlic to the pot, bring to a boil over medium-high heat, and continue to boil for 15 to 20 minutes. Pour into small sterilized bottles and seal. Allow to rest 2 weeks before using. Will last about a year once opened.

CURRY POWDER.

ONE ounce turmeric, one do. coriander seed, one do. cummin seed, one do. white ginger, one of nutmeg, one of mace, and one of Cayenne pepper; pound all together, and pass them through a line sieve; bottle and cork it well—one tea-spoonful is sufficient to season any made dish.

Randolph's Spice Mix

MAKES 7 OUNCES

In her description of her recipe Dish of Rice to be Served up with the Curry, In a Dish by Itself (not included in this volume), Randolph praises the usefulness of curry spices, noting, "Curry powder is used as a fine-flavored seasoning for fish, fowls, steaks, chops, veal cutlets, hashes, minces, alamodes, turtle soup, and in all rich dishes, gravies, sauce, &c. &c."

1 ounce turmeric

1 ounce coriander

1 ounce cumin

1 ounce ginger

1 ounce nutmeg

1 ounce mace

1 ounce cayenne
   pepper

Pound the ingredients together, or crush them in a blender or food processor for a few seconds.

Keep in a lidded container for up to 2 years.

Mary Randolph
AND HER LEGACY

The subtitle to Randolph's cookbook, *Method is the Soul of Management*, strikes a theme that runs throughout the work. Randolph did not just mean method in food production, although that may be part of her intent. She had a larger vision in mind. In her preface, she wrote, "The grand Arcanum of management lies in three simple rules:–'Let every thing be done at the proper time, keep every thing in its proper place, and put every thing to its proper place.'"[1] Randolph's rules emphasize organization and economy of movement, foreshadowing the work of social reformer Catherine Beecher and following the French cooking system *mise en place*.[2] Perhaps because of her personal experience, Randolph preached financial economy as well, offering advice of how to reuse leftover roast in A Nice Little Dish of Beef, and leftover breads with puddings and bread fritters.[3]

Her book complete, Randolph at first had difficulty finding a publisher for *The Virginia Housewife*, but finally, the Washington, DC, firm of Davis and Force printed it. A lithographer named Henry Stone, who may have financed the project, took out the copyright. Although her name did not appear on the title page of the first edition, Molly was credited as M. Randolph at the end of the preface.[4] *The Virginia Housewife* was an instant success. But soon after the cookbook appeared in 1824, tragedy struck the Randolph family. Molly and David's youngest son Burwell Starke Randolph, a midshipman in the US Navy, fell from a mast to the deck of his ship, permanently injuring his legs. Molly devoted her life to caring for her youngest child, nursing him back to health. Still, she found the time to produce a second edition of the widely popular cookbook.

The 1825 edition contained "amendments and additions," including additional recipes and three inserts illustrating place settings and inventions, including a bath water heater and a "refrigerator" or icebox that would have been extremely useful with Randolph's ice cream recipes. Her basic design was still in use until the development of electric refrigerators.[5] With his inventive mind, David may have assisted in the development of the inventions and the production of the illustrations.

Perhaps in an attempt to help market the new edition, Randolph sent a copy to former President James Madison in 1825, suggesting in an accompanying letter, "I shall be much flattered to know that you think it not intirely without merit."[6] In his response, Madison explained that while he felt ill equipped

Mary Randolph Grave, Arlington National Cemetery, Arlington, Virginia. Photo courtesy of Greta and Quinn Bledsoe.

to judge the merits of her book personally, he anticipated "the welcome reception that will be given to it by better judges than myself."[7]

Randolph was working on the third edition of *The Virginia Housewife* when she died January 23, 1828, at the age of sixty-five. Her son William Beverly Randolph received the copyright only three days before her death. This "enlarged" edition only included six new recipes, but it is possible that Randolph had intended to make additional changes.[8]

At her request, Mary Randolph's body was interred at Arlington, "in a spot marked out by herself." Her grave was the first one known on the estate that later became the site of Arlington National Cemetery. It is located about one hundred feet from the house, surrounded by a brick wall her cousins built "to keep the cattle away."[9] According to the epitaph carved into the flat stone that covers her slightly raised grave, Molly died "a victim of maternal love and duty." It goes on to declare that, "her intrinsic worth needs no eulogium." David died just two years later.

Mary Randolph's work lived on after her death. Through its numerous editions it taught Southern cuisine to thousands of cooks across the United States and became the standard of cooking for generations. Looking back at her childhood before the Civil War, Letitia M. Burwell, a member of another prominent Virginia family, recalled, "Every Virginia housewife knew how to compound all the various dishes in Mrs. Randolph's cookery book, and our tables were filled with every species of meat and vegetable to be found on a plantation, with every kind of cakes, jellies, and blanc-mange to be concocted out of eggs, butter, and cream, besides an endless catalogue of preserves, sweetmeats, pickles, and condiments."[10] And it was not just women who knew Randolph's work. Mrs. Mann Page relied heavily on the skills of her African-American butler George Orris: "It was only necessary to say to him that a certain number of guests were looked for to dinner, and everything would be done in a style to suit the occasion. George himself was said to know by heart every recipe in Mrs. Randolph's cookery-book, having been trained by that lady herself."[11] Simply put, Mary Randolph succeeded in producing the most significant American cookbook of the nineteenth century.[12] But as the century came to a close, *The Virginia Housewife* faded from the popular mind.

Interest in Mary Randolph revived in the twentieth century through unusual circumstances. In 1929 during a restoration of the mansion, War Department employees at Arlington National Cemetery grew curious about her grave, not knowing who she was or what her connection was to the estate. A story on the gravesite ran in *The Washington Star*, eliciting responses from members of the Randolph family.[13] Interest in Randolph and her work took off. Scholars began to study her contributions to American cooking, and the renewed attention led to the publication of at least four facsimile editions of *The Virginia Housewife*.[14] But still, even with all the renewed interest and scholarship, no cookbook attempted to update Mary Randolph's classic work using standard temperatures and measures and modern ingredients—until now.

Citrus Apple Pie

Chapter 4

BREADS,
DESSERTS, ETC.

PUDDINGS, ETC.

FONDUS.

PUT a pint of water, and a lump of butter the size of an egg, into a sauce pan; stir in as much flour as will make a thick batter, put it on the fire, and stir it continually till it will not stick to the pan; put it in a bowl, add three quarters of a pound of grated cheese, mix it well, then break in two eggs, beat them well, then two more until you put in six; when it looks very light, drop it in small lumps on buttered paper, bake it in a quick oven till of a delicate brown; you may use corn meal instead of flour for a change.

Cheese Puffs

MAKES 3 DOZEN

Cheese Puffs or gougères au fromage, *are light, airy pastries that rely on steam during the baking process to make them rise. Do not open the oven door while baking, as this might cause them to deflate.*

2 tablespoons butter, melted

¾ teaspoon salt

1 cup flour or cornmeal

4 eggs, beaten

1½ cups grated sharp cheddar cheese

In a medium saucepan, bring 1 cup water to boil at medium-high heat.

Reduce heat to medium-low and add butter and salt. Add flour and stir constantly until it forms into a ball.

Remove from heat and stir in eggs one at a time, until the dough is smooth, then stir in cheese.

Preheat oven to 425°F.

Line a baking sheet with parchment paper.

Drop the batter by tablespoonsful onto a sheet pan and bake for 15 to 20 minutes, until puffs are golden brown. Repeat until all the batter is used.

TO MAKE PUFF PASTE.

SIFT a quart of flour, leave out a little for rolling the paste, make up the remainder with cold water into a stiff paste, knead it well, and roll it out several times; wash the salt from a pound of butter, divide it into four parts, put one of them on the paste in little bits, fold it up, and continue to roll it till the butter is well mixed; then put another portion of butter, roll it in the same manner; do this till all the butter is mingled with the paste; touch it very lightly with the hands in making—bake it in a moderate oven, that will permit it to rise, but will not make it brown. Good paste must look white, and as light as a feather.

Puff Pastry

MAKES 1 SHEET (ABOUT 1 POUND)

Puff pastry is a light, flakey, buttery pastry used to make croissants and crusts for any variety of dishes. The key is the repeated folding and chilling.

1 cup flour, sifted

8 tablespoons (1 stick) unsalted butter, frozen

Plastic wrap

Lightly knead together the flour and ¼ cup cold water.

Coarsely grate the butter and cut it into the pastry. Wrap the pastry in plastic and refrigerate for 30 minutes.

On a floured surface, roll the pastry out into a rectangle about ½ inch thick. Fold in thirds like a letter. Rewrap and refrigerate for another 30 minutes.

Roll out again, fold, and refrigerate 2 more times. On the final time, chill for 1 hour. If not ready to use, place pastry in a tightly sealed container. It may be refrigerated for several days or frozen for 1 month before using.

TO MAKE MINCEMEAT
FOR PIES.

BOIL either calves or hogs' feet till perfectly tender, rub them through a colander; when cold, pass them through again, and it will come out like pearl barley; take one quart of this, one of chopped apples, the same of currants, washed and picked, raisins stoned and cut, of good brown sugar, suet nicely chopped, and cider, with a pint of brandy; add a tea-spoonful of pounded mace, one of cloves and of nutmegs; mix all these together intimately. When the pies are to be made, take out as much of this mixture as may be necessary; to each quart of it, add a tea-spoonful of pounded black pepper, and one of salt; this greatly improves the flavour, and can be better mixed with a small portion than with the whole mass. Cover the moulds with paste, put in a sufficiency of mince-meat, cover the top with citron sliced thin, and lay on it a lid garnished around with paste cut in fanciful shapes. They may be eaten either hot or cold, but are best when hot.

Mincemeat Pie

SERVES 8

Mincemeat, brought to Europe by Crusaders, originally consisted of dried fruits and various meats—suet, beef, mutton, and venison—mixed with wines and vinegars and baked into pies. It fell out of favor during the English Civil War (1642–1651), when the Puritans (who outlawed the celebration of Christmas) took control of England. Largely regarded as a country dish during the eighteenth century, it returned to popularity as a Christmas dessert during the Victorian era. By that time, the wines and vinegars had been replaced by brandy and the meat was gone, except for suet. Mincemeat can also be made using vegetable shortening as a substitute for the suet.

2 cups apples, diced

2 cups currants

2 cups raisins

2 cups dark brown sugar

2 cups suet, chopped (may substitute shortening)

1 cup cider

1 cup brandy

½ teaspoon mace

½ teaspoon cloves

½ teaspoon nutmeg

½ teaspoon salt

½ teaspoon pepper

1 citron, thinly sliced (may substitute 2 lemons)

Double Pastry Shell (see page 73)

Add all the ingredients except brandy and citron slices, and mix well in large pot. Bring to boil, stirring constantly. Reduce heat and simmer uncovered for two hours, string occasionally. Let cool. Stir in brandy. Cover with plastic wrap and refrigerate overnight.

When you are ready to bake the pies, Preheat oven to 400°F.

Prepare the pastry shells.

Pour the mincemeat into pastry shell and top with citron slices before covering with second pastry.

Crimp the edges of the pastry shells to close.

Bake for 40 to 45 minutes or until brown. Serve.

TO MAKE AN ORANGE PUDDING.

PUT two oranges and two lemons, into five quarts of water—boil them till the rinds are quite tender; take them out, and when cold, slice them thin, and pick out the seeds; put a pound of loaf sugar into a pint of water—when it boils, slice into it twelve pippins pared and cored—lay in the lemons and oranges, stew them tender, cover the dish with puff paste, lay the fruit in carefully, in alternate layers—pour on the syrup, put some slips of paste across, and bake it.

Citrus Apple Pie

SERVES 6

Pudding in Great Britain can either be used as a general word for a sweet dessert, or refer to any number of specific sweet or savory dishes often cooked by boiling in a bag. In this instance, Randolph's recipe describes a pie baked in a pastry crust.

1 large orange, whole unpeeled

1 large lemon, whole unpeeled

2¼ cups sugar

6 apples, peeled and sliced

Puff Pastry shell and strips of dough (see page 171)

1 tablespoon cornstarch (optional)

In a pot over high heat, boil the whole unpeeled orange and lemon in enough water to cover for 30 minutes. Allow the fruit to cool, then slice thinly, and seed.

Preheat oven to 375°F.

Prepare the Puff Pastry shell and dough strips.

Combine the sugar with 1½ cups water in a saucepan over medium-high heat, bring to a boil, stirring, and reduce the heat to medium. Add the apple slices and cook for 10 minutes. Add the orange and lemon slices and simmer for 30 to 40 minutes, or until tender. If the juice is runny, stir in 1 tablespoon cornstarch and mix well to thicken.

Pour the mixture into a pastry shell. Weave the strips of dough into a lattice top, and bake for 40 to 45 minutes, until the pastry begins to brown.

AN APPLE CUSTARD.

PARE and core twelve pippins, slice them tolerably thick, put a pound of loaf sugar in a stew pan, with a pint of water and twelve cloves: boil and skim it, then put in the apples, and stew them till clear, and but little of the syrup remains—lay them in a deep dish, and take out the cloves; when the apples are cold, pour in a quart of rich boiled custard—set it in water, and make it boil till the custard is set—take care the water does not get into it.

Apple Custard

SERVES 12

Custards are dishes made of milk thickened by eggs that have been popular in Europe since Ancient Rome. While Randolph prepared her custard using a boiling method in an oven, the modern version of the recipe calls for a simpler stovetop method.

3¼ cups sugar, divided

1 teaspoon ground cloves

6 large apples, pared, cored, and sliced

4 cups whole milk

8 egg yolks

Add 2 cups water, 2¼ cups sugar, and the cloves to a saucepot and bring to a low boil over medium-high heat, stirring continuously. Add the apples and continue to boil for 10 minutes, until thickened. Pour into a lightly greased, deep baking dish and allow to cool.

In the top of a double boiler over medium heat, warm the milk.

In a bowl, whisk together the egg yolks and remaining 1 cup sugar. Add this to the warm milk in the double boiler and heat, stirring constantly, until the liquid is thick enough to coat a spoon.

Pour over the apples, do not mix, and refrigerate, covered, 1 hour until set.

SWEET POTATO PUDDING.

BOIL one pound of sweet potatos very tender, rub them while hot through a colander; add six eggs well beaten, three quarters of a pound of powdered sugar, three quarters of butter, and some grated nutmeg and lemon peel, with a glass of brandy; put a paste in the dish, and when the pudding is done, sprinkle the top with sugar, and cover it with bits of citron. Irish potato pudding is made in the same manner, but is not so good.

Sweet Potato Pie

SERVES 8

For this "pudding" Randolph is again describing a pie, although this time open-faced. She uses the word paste *for the pie crust.*

1 Pastry Shell (see page 171)

1 pound sweet potatoes, peeled and grated

¾ cup cups sugar

½ cup butter

¾ cup whole milk

2 eggs, beaten

½ cup brandy

½ teaspoon nutmeg

1 teaspoon grated lemon peel

Powdered sugar, for sprinkling

2 ounces dried citron, chopped

Prepare the Pastry Shell.

Place grated sweet potatoes in a large saucepan. Cover with water and bring to boil on medium-high heat. Boil for 10 minutes, then drain.

In a large bowl, combine the sweet potatoes, sugar, butter, and milk. Add the eggs, one at a time, beating well after each egg. Stir in the brandy, nutmeg, and lemon peel.

Preheat oven to 325°F.

Pour mixture into the prepared Pastry Shell and bake for 45 to 60 minutes. The pie is done when a toothpick inserted in the center comes out clean.

Sprinkle with powdered sugar and dried citron and serve.

RICE PUDDING.

BOIL half a pound of rice in milk, until it is quite tender; beat it well with a wooden spoon to mash the grains; add three quarters of a pound of sugar, and the same of melted butter; half a nutmeg, six eggs, a gill of wine, and some grated lemon peel; put a paste in the dish, and bake it. For change, it may be boiled, and eaten with butter, sugar, and wine.

Southern Rice Pie

SERVES 6

Experiments in rice production began in Virginia in 1609, just two years after the establishment of Jamestown. The South Carolina and Georgia colonies became wealthy through the sale of rice during the colonial period using technology developed in the Senegambia region of West Africa.

1 Pastry Shell (see page 171)

2 cups whole milk

8 tablespoons (1 stick) butter

½ cup uncooked rice

¾ cup sugar

2 eggs

⅛ teaspoon nutmeg

2 ounces white wine

½ teaspoon grated lemon peel

Prepare the Pastry Shell.

Preheat oven to 350°F.

Scald the milk in a saucepot over medium heat, but do not bring to a boil. Add butter. Stir in the rice, reduce the heat to medium-low, and cook for 25 to 30 minutes, or until the rice is tender. Mash well with potato masher or whip in blender or food processor.

In a bowl, stir together the sugar, eggs, nutmeg, and wine and add this to the pot of rice.

Pour into the Pastry Shell and bake for 20 to 30 minutes, until top is brown.

ALMOND PUDDING.

PUT a pound of sweet almonds in hot water till the skin will slip off
them; pound them with a little orange flower or rose water, to keep them
from oiling; mix with them four crackers, finely pounded, or two gills
of rice flour; six eggs, a pint of cream, a pound of sugar, half a pound of
butter, and four table-spoonsful of wine; put a nice paste in the bottom of
your dish, garnish the edges, pour in the pudding bake it in a moderate
oven.

Almond Tart

SERVES 8

Almond meal is available online if it is difficult to locate in local stores, or you can make it by grinding almonds in a food processer. Tarts can be baked in a tart pan, a nine-inch round cake pan, or a large pie pan.

1 Pastry Shell (see page 171)

1¾ cups almond meal, or ½ pound almonds, ground

1 teaspoon orange extract, or ½ tablespoon rose water (may substitute 1 teaspoon orange liquor for orange extract or 1 teaspoon vanilla extract for rose water)

2 graham crackers, grated

½ cup rice flour

2 eggs

1 cup cream

1 cup sugar

8 tablespoons (1 stick) butter

¼ cup sweet white wine

Prepare a Pastry Shell.

Preheat oven to 350°F.

Mix the almond meal in a large bowl with orange extract or rose water. Add the remaining ingredients and stir well.

Pour into an unbaked pastry shell and bake for 15 to 30 minutes. This tart is very nice topped with whipped cream or served warm with ice cream.

LEMON PUDDING.

GRATE the rind from six fresh lemons, squeeze the juice from three, and strain it; beat the yelks of sixteen eggs very light, put to them sixteen table-spoonsful of powdered loaf sugar, not heaped up—the same of melted butter; add the grated rind, and the juice, four crackers finely pounded, or an equal quantity of rice flour; or for change, six ounces of corn meal which is excellent—beat it till light, put a puff paste in your dish, pour the pudding in, and bake it in a moderate oven—it must not be very brown.

Lemon Tart

SERVES 8

Although some wealthy Virginia planters made attempts to grow citrus fruit in greenhouses or orangeries, most citrus was imported to the mainland colonies from islands in the Caribbean. Serving citrus at the table would have demonstrated great wealth and sophistication.

1 Puff Pastry
(see page 171)

6 lemons

12 egg yolks, beaten

1 cup sugar

1 cup melted butter

4 graham crackers, grated, or 6 ounces cornmeal

Prepare Puff Pastry Shell.

Preheat oven to 350°F.

In a small bowl, grate the rind of the lemons, and add the juice of 3 lemons, removing the seeds.

In a separate bowl, beat the egg yolks 2 to 3 minutes, and stir in the sugar, butter, and crackers. Add the lemon rind and juice to this and stir well to combine.

Pour into the pastry shell and bake for 30 to 40 minutes.

BAKED APPLE PUDDING.

TAKE well flavoured apples, bake, but do not burn them, rub them through a sieve, take one pound of the apples so prepared, mix with it, while hot, half a pound of butter, and half a pound of powdered sugar; the rinds of two lemons grated—and when cold, add six eggs well beaten; put a paste in the bottom of a dish, and pour in the apples—half an hour will bake it; sift a little sugar on the apples when baked.

Apple Tart

SERVES 6

Virginians had hundreds of varieties of apples from which to choose when preparing food. Thomas Jefferson grew eighteen different varieties at Monticello.

1 Pastry Shell, uncooked (see page 171)

1 pound apples, peeled, cored, and cut into slices

1 cup sugar, plus more for sprinkling after baking

¼ cup (1 stick) butter

4 eggs, beaten

2 teaspoons grated lemon peel

Prepare the Pastry Shell.

Preheat the oven to 350°F.

Place apples in a greased casserole dish and bake 40 to 50 minutes until tender.

Press the apples through a sieve or run through a food processor.

Combine all remaining ingredients, mix well, and pour into the pastry shell. Bake for 30 to 40 minutes. Sprinkle with sugar before serving.

BAKED INDIAN
MEAL PUDDING.

BOIL one quart of milk, mix in it two gills and a half of corn meal very smoothly, eggs well beaten, a gill of molasses, and a good piece of butter, bake it two hours.

Crustless Cornmeal Pie

SERVES 8

Cornmeal Pie has a nutty flavor similar to pecan pie. Randolph might have been alluding to Native American origins when she referred to cornmeal as Indian Meal in her title.

1¼ cups cornmeal

4 cups whole milk

½ cup molasses

5 eggs, beaten

2 tablespoons butter, melted

Preheat oven to 325°F.

Combine the cornmeal and milk in the top of a double boiler over medium heat and cook, stirring occasionally, for 15 minutes. Add the molasses and eggs, and cook another 5 minutes, stirring occasionally, then remove from heat and stir in the butter.

Pour the batter into a well greased baking dish or pie plate and bake for 1½ to 2 hours.

POTATO PASTE.

BOIL mealy potatos quite soft, first taking off the skins; rub them while hot through a sieve, put them in a stew pan over the fire, with as much water as will make it the consistence of thick mush; sift one quart of flour, and make it into a paste; with this mush, knead it till light, roll it out thin, make the dumplins small—fill them with apples, or any other fruit—tie them up in a thick cloth, and boil them nicely—eat them with butter, sugar, and nutmeg.

Fruit Dumplings

MAKES 8

You will need enough cheesecloth to wrap each apple or pear in an individual square for cooking.

2 large potatoes, peeled and boiled

4 cups flour

8 apples or pears, peeled and cored

2 tablespoons butter, melted

½ cup sugar

¼ teaspoon nutmeg

Grate the cooked potatoes into a saucepot. Stir in ½ cup water and warm over low heat, stirring until the mixture is mushy.

Transfer to a large bowl. Sift in the flour and knead it until the dough holds together in a ball. Divide the pastry into 8 equal portions and roll each into a 6-inch circle.

Moisten the edge of each circle with water and place 1 apple or pear into each. Wrap the pastry around the fruit.

Bring a large pot of lightly salted water to a gentle boil.

Cut 8 (10-inch) squares of cheesecloth. Wrap each dumpling in a cloth square and secure with cooking twine. Drop them in the gently boiling water, and cook for 35 to 40 minutes.

Remove the dumplings from water and discard the cheesecloth. Place each dumpling into individual serving bowls.

Place the melted butter in a shallow bowl. Stir in the sugar and nutmeg until well combined, and pour over dumplings. Serve immediately.

COMPOTE OF APPLES.

PARE and core the apples, and if you prefer it, cut them in four, wash them clean, and put them in a pan with water and sugar enough to cover them; add cinnamon and lemon peel, which has been previously soaked, scraped on the inside, and cut in strings; boil them gently until the apples are done, take them out in a deep dish, boil the syrup to a proper consistency, and pour it on them: it will take a pound of sugar for a large dish.

Apple Compote

SERVES 8

Compote is a dish developed in the Middle East consisting of fruit stewed in simple syrup. During the Middle Ages, fruit compote became an important part of celebratory feasts in England.

8 apples, pared, cored, and quartered

½ cup sugar

1 tablespoon grated lemon peel

1 teaspoon cinnamon

Add the apples and sugar to a saucepan along with enough water to cover. Cook over medium-high heat just until the water begins to boil, then reduce the heat to low and simmer for 15 to 20 minutes until the apples have cooked down, but maintain some form. Transfer the apples to a serving dish, retaining the liquid in the pot.

To the liquid in the pot, add the lemon peel and cinnamon and cook over medium heat to thicken, stirring constantly. Pour over the apples. This dish may be served either warm or cold.

APPLE FRITTERS.

PARE some apples, and cut them in thin slices—put them in a bowl, with a glass of brandy, some white wine, a quarter of a pound of pounded sugar, a little cinnamon finely powdered, and the rind of a lemon grated; let them stand some time, turning them over frequently; beat two eggs very light, add one quarter of a pound of flour, a table-spoonful of melted butter, and as much cold water as will make a thin batter; drip the apples on a sieve, mix them with the batter, take one slice with a spoonful of batter to each fritter, fry them quickly of a light brown, drain them well, put them in a dish, sprinkling sugar over each, and glaze them nicely.

Southern Apple Fritters

SERVES 8

Modern apple fritters are similar to doughnuts with diced fruit in the dough, unlike their historic forebears, which are fried battered apple slices.

8 apples, peeled, cored, and thinly sliced

⅓ cup brandy

½ cup white wine

¼ cup sugar

½ teaspoon cinnamon

1½ teaspoons grated lemon peel

2 eggs, beaten

1 cup flour

1 tablespoon butter, melted

2 tablespoons cooking oil

½–¾ cup powdered sugar

Marinate the apple slices in a bowl with the brandy, wine, sugar, cinnamon, and lemon peel for 1 hour, stirring occasionally. Pour into a colander to drain excess liquid.

In a bowl, mix together the eggs, flour, butter, and ½ cup cold water. Mix the apples into this batter.

Heat the oil in a skillet over medium-high heat. Drop tablespoonsful of batter (each containing 1 apple slice) into the hot oil and fry until golden brown, about 4 to 5 minutes per side. Remove with a slotted spoon and transfer to paper towels or baking rack to drain. Sprinkle well with powdered sugar. Best served warm.

CAKES.

JUMBALS.

PUT one pound of nice sugar into two pounds of flour, add pounded spice of any kind, and pass them through a sieve; beat four eggs, pour them on with three quarters of a pound of melted butter, knead all well together, and bake them.

Cinnamon Jumbals

MAKES 2–3 DOZEN

Jumbals are cookies or teacakes that were traditionally formed in a love knot, but they can be rolled and cut in any shape, as in this modern version of the recipe. For a more traditional jumbal, take a heaping teaspoon of batter and roll it into a rope. Form into a circle or tie into a knot before baking.

3½ cups flour

1 cup sugar

1 teaspoon cinnamon

2 eggs

¾ melted butter

Preheat oven to 350°F.

In a large bowl, sift together the flour, sugar, and cinnamon.

In a separate bowl, beat the eggs and stir in the butter. Knead this egg mixture into the flour mixture to form a dough.

On a floured surface, roll the dough out very thin. Cut in desired shapes and bake 10 to 12 minutes, until brown.

MACAROONE.

BLANCH a pound of sweet almonds, pound them in a mortar with rose water; whip the whites of seven eggs to a strong froth, put in one pound of powdered sugar, beat it some time, then put in the almonds—mix them well, and drop them on sheets of paper buttered; sift sugar over, and bake them quickly. Be careful not to let them get discoloured.

Almond Macaroons

MAKES 1 DOZEN

Macaroon cookies were developed in Italy in the eighth or ninth century. The name originates from the Italian word ammaccare, *meaning to crush. An alternative to grating the almonds is to simply run them through a food processor.*

2 egg whites

1 cup powdered sugar

1 cup grated almonds, or almond flour

¼ cup granulated sugar

Preheat oven to 350°F.

Beat egg whites with powdered sugar until very stiff. Stir in the grated almonds and mix until smooth. Drop by the spoonful onto a parchment paper-lined sheet pan. Sprinkle with granulated sugar. Bake for 10 to 12 minutes, or until the cookies are firm and golden.

TAVERN BISCUIT.

TO one pound of flour, add half a pound of sugar, half a pound of butter, some mace and nutmeg powdered, and a glass of brandy or wine; wet it with milk, and when well kneaded, roll it thin, cut it in shapes, and bake it quickly.

Tavern Cookies

MAKES APPROXIMATELY 2 DOZEN COOKIES

In British English biscuit *refers to a crisp cookie, such as this recipe. American English adopted the word* cookie *from the Dutch who settled New Netherlands, later known as New York. The number of cookies in this recipe depends greatly on the size of the cookie cutters used.*

3½ cups flour

1 cup sugar

½ teaspoon mace

1 teaspoon nutmeg

½ pound butter, room temperature

½ cup brandy or white wine

Milk, as needed

Preheat oven to 350°F.

In a large bowl, sift together the flour, sugar, mace, and nutmeg. Cut in the butter. Add the brandy and a little milk and combine to make a soft dough, adding more milk as needed.

Roll the dough out on a floured surface ¼ to ½-inch thick, and cut into desired shapes. Bake on a greased cookie sheet for 10 to 12 minutes or until brown.

PLEBEIAN GINGER BREAD.

MIX three large spoonsful of pounded ginger, with three quarts of flour—
sift it, dissolve three tea-spoonsful of pearl-ash in a cup of water, and
pour it on the flour; melt half a pound of butter in a quart of molasses,
mix it with the flour, knead it well, cut it in shapes, and bake it.

Gingerbread Cookies

MAKES APPROXIMATELY 1½ DOZEN COOKIES

Pearl ash, the name for potassium carbonate, is made by refining salts of tarter, and was commercially available before baking powder was commercially produced in the middle of the nineteenth century.

2½ cups flour

1½ teaspoon ground ginger

½ cup butter, melted

½ cup molasses

1 teaspoon baking soda

Preheat oven to 350°F.

In a medium bowl, sift the flour and ginger together.

In a separate bowl, melt the butter and stir in the molasses.

In another bowl, stir the baking soda into ⅓ cup water.

Cut the molasses and the soda into the flour, and knead well.

Roll the dough out on a floured surface and cut into desired shapes.

Bake on greased baking sheet for 8 to 10 minutes.

SUGAR GINGER BREAD.

TAKE two pounds of the nicest brown sugar, dry and pound it, put it into three quarts of flour, add a large cup full of powdered ginger, and sift the mixture; wash the salt out of a pound of butter, and cream it; have twelve eggs well beaten; work into the butter first, the mixture, then the froth from the eggs, until all are in, and it is quite light; add a glass of brandy butter shallow moulds, pour it in, and bake in a quick oven.

Sugar Ginger Cake

SERVES 10

Like Savoy Cake (see page 209), this ginger cake relies on eggs to rise. Bring the eggs to room temperature before using and whip them extremely well. Do not open the oven door during baking; otherwise the cake will fall.

3 cups flour

¾ cup dark brown sugar, tightly packed

¼ cup ground ginger

8 tablespoons (1 stick) unsalted butter, room temperature

3 eggs

2 tablespoons brandy

Preheat oven to 400°F.

Sift the flour in a large bowl. Cut in the brown sugar and ginger.

Cream the butter and cut it into the flour.

Beat the eggs to a good froth and blend into the butter/flour mixture. Stir in the brandy.

Spoon into a well-greased pan and bake for 35 to 40 minutes, or until a toothpick comes out clean. (Cut the baking time in half if using baking molds.)

RISEN CAKE.

TAKE three pounds of flour, one and a half of pounded sugar, a tea-spoonful of cloves, one of mace, and one of ginger, all finely powdered—pass the whole through a sieve, put to it four spoonsful of good yeast, and twelve eggs—mix it up well, and if not sufficiently soft, add a little milk: make it up at night, and set it to rise—when well risen, knead into it a pound of butter, and two gills of brandy; have ready two pounds of raisins stoned, mix all well together, pour it into a mould of proper size, and bake it in an oven heated as for bread; let it stand till thoroughly done, and do not take it from the mould until quite cold.

Raisin Bundt Cake

SERVES 10

Early cakes in England were essentially breads using yeast as a leavening agent. These had fallen out of favor by the middle of the eighteenth century, when bakers relied on eggs to make the dough rise, and in the nineteenth century as carbonates began to take over, first with pearl ash, then baking soda, and finally baking powder.

3½ cups flour

1 package or 2¼ teaspoons yeast

1 cup sugar

¼ teaspoon cloves

¼ teaspoon mace

¼ teaspoon ginger

3 eggs, well beaten

Milk, to soften the dough

⅔ cup butter, softened

⅓ cup brandy

1 cup raisins

In a large bowl, sift together the flour, yeast, sugar, cloves, mace, and ginger. Stir in the eggs and a little milk, and knead, adding milk as needed to make a soft dough. Place the dough in a greased bowl, cover bowl with damp cloth, and let it sit out overnight—it will almost double in size.

The next day, knead in the butter, brandy, and raisins.

Preheat oven to 400°F.

Grease and flour a bundt pan. Stir the batter and pour into the pan. Let the batter rise 1 hour.

Reduce the oven heat to 350°F, and bake for an additional 35 to 40 minutes or until a toothpick comes out clean.

Let cool before removing from pan.

SAVOY OR SPUNGE CAKE.

TAKE twelve fresh eggs, put them in the scale, and balance them with sugar: take out half, and balance the other half with flour; separate the whites from the yelks, whip them up very light, then mix them, and sift in, first sugar, then flour, till both are exhausted; add some grated lemon peel; bake them in paper cases, or little tin moulds. This also makes an excellent pudding, with butter, sugar, and wine, for sauce.

Savoy Sponge Cake

SERVES 8

Savoy is the region of Europe where Italy, France, and Switzerland meet. The cake that developed there in the seventeenth century took Europe by storm. Like a soufflé, it relies on whipped eggs to rise instead of yeast or soda. And like a soufflé, it can fall quite easily. There are three tricks to making a successful Savoy cake. Remove the eggs from the refrigerator an hour in advance to bring them up to room temperature. Whip them extremely well. And do not open the oven door to check on the cake before the time is up. Otherwise, the cake is likely to collapse.

6 eggs, separated

2 cups sugar, sifted

2 cups flour, sifted

1 tablespoon grated lemon peel

Unsalted butter, to grease the pan

Preheat oven to 350°F.

In a large bowl, beat the egg yolks for 2 to 3 minutes, then fold in the sugar.

In a separate bowl, beat the egg whites until stiff.

Sift the flour into another bowl.

Alternating, fold ⅓ egg whites, then ⅓ flour into yolk mixture, stirring well after each addition. Repeat until all egg whites and flour are mixed into batter.

Stir in the grated lemon peel.

Use unsalted butter to grease cake molds or cupcake pans. If using cupcake pans or small molds, bake 20 to 25 minutes. If pouring the batter into a bundt, tube, or large mold, bake 45 to 50 minutes, or until a toothpick comes out clean.

A RICH FRUIT CAKE.

HAVE the following articles prepared, before you begin the cake: four
pounds of flour dried and sifted, four pounds of butter washed to free
it from salt, two pounds of loaf sugar pounded, a quarter of a pound of
mace, the same of nutmegs powdered; wash four pounds of currants
clean, pick and dry them; blanch one pound of sweet almonds, and cut
them in very thin slices; stone two pounds of raisins, cut them in two,
and strew a little flour over to prevent their sticking together, and two
pounds of citron sliced thin; break thirty eggs, separating the yelks and
whites; work the butter to a cream with your hand-put in alternately,
flour, sugar, and the froth from both whites and yelks, which must be
beaten separately, and only the froth put in. When all are mixed and
the cake looks very light, add the spice, with half a pint of brandy, the
currants and almonds; butter the mould well, pour in part of the cake,
strew over it some raisins and citron—do this until all is in: set it in a
well heated oven: when it has risen, and the top is coloured, cover it with
paper; it will require three hours baking—it must be iced.

Rich Fruitcake

SERVES 16

A very dense cake, fruitcake can be baked in loaf pans or molds. For those who are counting, Randloph's original recipe calls for nine pounds of fruits and nuts.

3 cups flour, divided

8 eggs, separated

1¾ cups unsalted butter

1 cup sugar

½ cup brandy

3 tablespoons mace

3 tablespoons nutmeg

⅔ cup almond slivers, blanched

¾ cup dried currants

1¼ cup raisins

½ cup candied citron

For the Glaze:

1½ cups powdered sugar

1 teaspoon vanilla extract

3–4 tablespoons milk

Preheat oven to 250°F.

Sift 2½ cups flour into a bowl

Beat egg yolks. Cream butter with egg yolks and sugar in a large bowl.

Beat egg whites until stiff.

Alternating, fold ⅓ egg whites and flour into yolk mixture, stirring well.

Stir in brandy and spices.

Toss nuts and fruits in a bowl with the remaining ½ cup flour and stir into the batter.

Grease and flour baking pan.

Pour the batter into the pan and bake for 2½ hours, then increase the heat to 300°F and bake an additional 15 minutes. Test with a knife to see if done. When cake has cooled, remove from pan.

To make the Glaze

Combine all ingredients and stir well. Pour over cooled cake.

SHREWSBURY CAKES.

MIX a pound of sugar, with two pounds of flour, and a large spoonful of pounded coriander seeds; sift them, add three quarters of a pound of melted butter, six eggs, and a gill of brandy; knead it well, roll it thin, cut it in shapes, and bake without discolouring it.

Shrewsbury Cookies

MAKES APPROXIMATELY 2 DOZEN

These buttery cookies were developed in the medieval town of Shrewsbury in Shropshire, a county in the West Midlands of England, bordering Wales.

1 cup sugar

3½ cups flour

1 teaspoon ground
   coriander

3 sticks
   (24 tablespoons)
   butter, melted

3 eggs, beaten

2 ounces brandy

Preheat oven to 300°F.

Sift together the sugar, flour and coriander in a large bowl. Stir in the melted butter, along with the eggs and brandy, and knead well.

Roll the dough out on a floured surface and cut into desired shapes.

Bake on greased baking sheet for 12 to 15 minutes.

LITTLE PLUM CAKES.

PREPARE them as directed for pound cake, add raisins and currants, bake them in small tin shapes, and ice them.

Raisin-Currant Cakes

SERVES 8

These wonderful cakes make a nice alternative to the heavier fruitcake during the holidays.

2 cups unsalted butter

2 cups sugar

10 eggs, separated

3½ cups flour, plus
    more as needed

2 teaspoons nutmeg

1 teaspoon grated
    lemon peel

½ cup brandy

1 cup raisins

1 cup currants

For the Glaze:

1½ cups powdered
    sugar

1 teaspoon vanilla
    extract

3-4 tablespoons milk

Preheat oven to 350°F.

Cream the butter and sugar together in a large bowl.

Beat the egg yolks and add them to the butter mixture.

In a separate bowl, sift together the flour and nutmeg. Slowly add the flour to the batter and stir until well blended.

Beat the egg whites until stiff and fold them into the batter.

Stir in the lemon peel and brandy.

Toss the raisins and currants in a bowl with a little flour to coat, and stir these into the batter.

Pour the batter into greased cake molds. Bake 40 to 50 minutes, or follow baking mold directions.

Remove cakes and let cool.

To make the Glaze

Combine all ingredients and stir well. Pour over the cooled cakes.

RICE BREAD.

BOIL six ounces of rice in a quart of water, till it is dry and soft—put it into two pounds of flour, mix it in well; add two tea-spoonsful of salt, two large spoonsful of yeast, and as much water as will make it the consistence of bread: when well risen, bake it in moulds.

Southern Rice Bread

SERVES 12

Rice bread was quite common in Georgia and South Carolina where rice was a staple crop. Because it was grown locally, it frequently was less expensive than wheat flour.

1 package, or
  2¼ teaspoons, yeast

1 cup cooked rice

½ teaspoon salt

5–7 cups flour

Dissolve yeast in a bowl with ½ cup warm water.

Add the rice and let stand in a warm place for 3 hours.

Add salt to the rice, and knead in flour a cup at a time to make a stiff dough.

Cover the dough and let it rise in a cool place until it doubles in size, typically about 45 minutes.

Punch the dough down and knead again. Cover and let rise again until doubled in size.

Preheat oven to 350°F.

Bake for 40 to 50 minutes, or until lightly browned. Slice and serve.

SWEET POTATO BUNS.

BOIL and mash a potato, rub into it as much flour as will make it like bread—add spice and sugar to your taste, with a spoonful of yeast; when it has risen well, work in a piece of butter, bake it in small rolls, to be eaten hot with butter, either for breakfast or tea.

Sweet Potato Yeast Rolls

MAKES APPROXIMATELY 2 DOZEN

Mashed sweet potatoes add a wonderful hint of color and texture to "boring" yeast rolls. To spice them up even further, add a quarter teaspoon nutmeg, cloves, and/or cinnamon.

1 package, or
  2¼ teaspoons, yeast

¼ cup sugar, divided

½ cup sweet potatoes,
  cooked, mashed

1 teaspoon salt

4 tablespoons butter,
  melted

3 cups flour

¼ teaspoon nutmeg,
  cloves and/or
  cinnamon (optional)

Preheat oven to 400°F.

Dissolve the yeast in a large bowl with ½ cup warm water and 1 tablespoon sugar. Let stand 5 minutes. Stir in the mashed sweet potatoes, salt, the remaining sugar, and the butter. Blend in the flour (and spices if desired) and knead 2 to 3 minutes. Shape into ball and place in a greased bowl. Cover and let rise one hour. Punch down. Divide into balls and place on greased cookie sheet. Let rise until doubled in size.

Roll out on a lightly floured surface and cut in desired shapes.

Bake on a greased sheet pan for 15 to 20 minutes.

TO MAKE CUSTARD.

MAKE a quart of milk quite hot, that it may not whey when baked; let it stand to get cold, and then mix six eggs with it; sweeten it with loaf sugar, and fill the custard cups—put on the covers, and set them in a Dutch oven with water, but not enough to risk its boiling into the cups; do not put on the top of the oven. When the water has boiled ten or fifteen minutes, take out a cup, and if the custard be the consistence of jelly; it is sufficiently done; serve them in the cups with the covers on, and a tea-spoon on the dish between each cup—grate nutmeg on the tops when cold.

Egg Custard

SERVES 6

Cooking custard in a pan of steaming water helps the custard to bake evenly, preventing the outside from baking before the center.

2 cups whole milk, scalded

4 eggs

½ cup sugar

1 teaspoon nutmeg

Preheat oven to 350°F.

Combine milk, eggs, and sugar and mix well. Pour into 6 custard cups and set them in a baking pan filled 1 inch deep with hot water. Bake for 30 to 35 minutes. Sprinkle with nutmeg before serving.

TO MAKE A TRIFLE.

PUT slices of Savoy cake or Naples biscuit at the bottom of a deep dish; wet it with white wine, and fill the dish nearly to the top with rich boiled custard; season half a pint of cream with white wine and sugar; whip it to a froth—as it rises, take it lightly off, and lay it on the custard; pile it up high and tastily—decorate it with preserves of any kind, cut so thin as not to bear the froth down by its weight.

Trifle

SERVES 10-12

Trifle became extremely popular in the South during the colonial period. Wealthy Southern ladies often had cut glass bowls specifically for displaying the layers of this elegant dessert.

Savoy Cake (see page 208), sliced 1 inch thick

1 cup white wine, divided

Custard (see page 221)

1 cup whipping cream

½ cup sugar

1 (15-ounce) jar preserves, your choice fruit

Line the bottom of a deep serving dish with slices of cake. Soak with ½ cup wine.

Pour the custard on top of the cake slices.

In a separate bowl, beat together the cream, sugar, and the remaining wine until frothy. With a cake spatula, add the cream mixture, and layer on in peaks.

Mix preserves with 1 cup water and drizzle onto the cream layer. Refrigerate at least 1 hour before serving.

COLD CREAMS.

 ## LEMON CREAM.

PARE the rind very thin from four fresh lemons, squeeze the juice, and strain it—put them both into a quart of water, sweeten it to your taste, add the whites of six eggs, beat to a froth; set it over the fire, and keep stirring until it thickens, but do not let it boil—then pour it in a bowl; when cold, strain it through a sieve, put it on the fire, and add the yelks of the eggs—stir it till quite thick, and serve it in glasses.

Lemon Pudding

SERVES 6

The category of dessert Randolph calls Cold Creams does not refer to ice cream, but something more like what Americans would refer to as puddings, although not as thick. This recipe for Lemon Pudding can be adapted to make Orange Pudding as well.

Zest and juice of 4 lemons

1 cup sugar

5 eggs, separated

In a saucepan over medium-low heat, add 1 quart water and the zest and juice. Stir in the sugar and egg whites and whip until frothy. Simmer, stirring constantly, for 10 minutes, or until it thickens. Remove from heat and pour through strainer to remove and discard the zest, then return the pudding to the saucepan.

Beat the egg yolks and add them to the pudding. Simmer another 10 minutes until thick, then pour into parfait glasses and refrigerate at least 1 hour before serving.

RASPBERRY CREAM.

STIR as much raspberry marmalade into a quart of cream, as will be sufficient to give a rich flavour of the fruit—strain it, and fill your glasses, leaving out a part to whip into froth for the top.

Raspberry Pudding

SERVES 6

This light, frothy dish is a perfect dessert to end a summer meal.

1 (15-ounce) jar seedless raspberry marmalade

4 cups cream

1 cup whipping cream

2 tablespoons sugar

Stir the marmalade to loosen, and pour into a bowl. Stir in the cream until well combined, and pour into 6 parfait glasses. Chill or freeze 1 hour.

Beat the whipping cream, adding the sugar a little at a time, and beat until stiff. Garnish each glass with a dollop of the whipped cream.

TEA CREAM.

PUT one ounce of the best tea in a pitcher, pour on it a table spoonful of water, and let it stand an hour to soften the leaves; then put to it a quart of boiling cream, cover it close, and in half an hour strain it; add four tea-spoonsful of a strong infusion of rennet in water, stir it, and set it on some hot ashes, and cover it; when you find by cooling a little of it, that it will jelly, pour it into glasses, and garnish with thin bits of preserved fruit.

Southern Tea Pudding

SERVES 4

Southerners' love affair with tea dates back to the colonial period when the tea ceremony was an important part of social behavior. Tea was used as flavoring in a number of drinks, including alcohol punches. In this recipe, Randolph uses it to flavor a dessert.

1 rennet tablet
   (or 1 tablespoon
   cornstarch)

½ cup **tea**, well
   steeped, and strong

2 cups cream

3 tablespoons sugar

Crush the rennet tablet and add 1 tablespoon cold water.

Combine with the remaining ingredients in a saucepan over low heat, and heat slowly until warm, stirring often.

Pour into 4 sherbet glasses. Let stand for a few minutes, then refrigerate for 1 hour before serving.

GOOSEBERRY FOOL.

PICK the stems and blossoms from two quarts of green gooseberries; put them in a stew pan, with their weight in loaf sugar, and a very little water—when sufficiently stewed, pass the pulp through a sieve; and when cold, add rich boiled custard till it is like thick cream; put it in a glass bowl, and lay frothed cream on the top.

Gooseberry Fool

SERVES 6

A fool *is a classic English dessert dating back to the Late Middle Ages, made by adding pureed, stewed fruit into an egg custard. It can be made using any variety of fruit, but gooseberry is traditional. While growing gooseberries has gone out of fashion, they are still available in specialty markets, online, and can even be found canned.*

1 pound or 1 (15-ounce) can gooseberries

2 cups, plus 2 tablespoons sugar

Egg Custard (see page 221)

1 cup whipping cream

Stew the gooseberries in a saucepan over medium heat with the 2 cups sugar and a little water for 5 minutes, or until tender.

Puree the gooseberries and stir gently into the custard. Pour into a glass serving bowl. Refrigerate at least 1 hour.

Whip the cream with the remaining 2 tablespoons sugar until stiff. Spread the whipped cream over the custard and serve.

BLANC MANGE.

BREAK one ounce of isinglass into very small pieces; wash it well, and pour on a pint of boiling water; next morning, add a quart of milk, boil it till the isinglass is dissolved, strain it, put in two ounces sweet almonds, blanched and pounded; sweeten it, and put it in the mould—when stiff, turn them into a deep dish, and put raspberry cream around them. For a change, stick thin slips of blanched almonds all over the blanc mange, and dress round with syllabub, nicely frothed. Some moulds require colouring—for an ear of corn, mix the yelk of an egg with a little of the blanc mange; fill the grains of the corn with it—and when quite set, pour in the white, but take care it is not warm enough to melt the yellow: for a bunch of asparagus, colour a little with spinach juice, to fill the green tops of the heads. Fruit must be made the natural colour of what it represents. Cochineal and alkanet root pounded and dissolved in brandy, make good colouring; but blanc mange should never be served, without raspberry cream or syllabub to eat with it.

Blancmange

SERVES 4

Blancmange is a gelatin dessert that dates back to the Middle Ages. It was a "performance" dessert in that it can be shaped into any number of whimsical forms.

1 cup whole milk, divided

1 (¼-ounce) packet gelatin

6 tablespoons sugar

1 cup cream

2 egg whites, whipped until slightly stiff

1 pinch salt

2 tablespoons grated, blanched almonds, plus more for a garnish

Pour ½ cup milk in a bowl. Sprinkle gelatin on top and let it rest for 10 minutes.

Heat the remaining ½ cup milk in a saucepan over medium heat and pour it over the gelatin.

Add the sugar and stir until it dissolves. Cover and refrigerate 1 hour, or until the mixture has slightly thickened.

Beat the mixture to incorporate air. Fold in the cream, the whipped egg whites, salt, and nuts. Pour into cups or a mold, cover tightly, and freeze until firm. Garnish with slivers of almond.

TO MAKE A HEN'S NEST.

GET five small eggs, make a hole at one end, and empty the shells—fill them with blanc mange: when stiff and cold, take off the shells, pare the yellow rind very thin from six lemons, boil them in water till tender, then cut them in thin strips to resemble straw, and preserve them with sugar; fill a small deep dish half full of nice jelly—when it is set, put the straw on in form of a nest, and lay the eggs in it. It is a beautiful dish for a dessert or supper.

Hen's Nest

SERVES 6

An example of the type of dish that can be made using blancmange, Randolph's whimsical creation makes for a "show-stopping" dessert.

For the Candied Lemon Peels:

6 lemons

Dash salt

2 cups sugar

For the Hen's Nest:

Blancmange
(see page 233)

To Prepare the Candied Lemon Peels

This should be done 2 days before you are going to serve this dessert.

Pare lemons in wide strips, avoiding as much pith as possible. Place peels in a saucepan cover with water, and bring to a boil over medium-high heat. Boil for 10 minutes, or until tender, and drain

Add the dash of salt to fresh water, bring to a boil, and boil the peel again for 5 minutes. Drain the peel and spread out on a parchment paper. Let dry overnight in a dry, cool place.

The next day, use kitchen scissors or a sharp paring knife to cut the rind into very thin strips.

Make a syrup with the sugar and 2 cups water in a saucepan over medium-high heat, stirring until the sugar has dissolved. Add the peel and bring to boil, then reduce heat to medium-low and simmer for 45 to 60 minutes or until peels are almost translucent.

Drain the peels and spread out on parchment paper. Let dry overnight in a dry, cool place.

The day you are serving this dish, prepare the Blancmange.

Pour Blancmange into egg-shaped molds to produce 3 or 4 eggs.

Pour remaining Blancmange into a 1-quart serving bowl.

Freeze Blancmange at least 1 hour until set. Remove eggs from mold and arrange on top of the blancmange in the bowl.

Cover the top of the Blancmange with the lemon peel to create the "nest," leaving eggs exposed.

Chill in refrigerator until ready to serve.

NOTES

Introduction

[1] Janice Bluestein Longone, "Introduction to the Dover Edition," in Mary Randolph, *The Virginia Housewife or, Methodical Cook: A Facsimile of an Authentic Early American Cookbook* (New York: Dover Publications, Inc., 1993), 3, 4; John L. Hess and Karen Hess, *The Taste of America* (Columbia: University of South Carolina Press, 1989), 89; and Harry Haff, *The Founders of American Cuisine* (Jefferson, NC: McFarland & Company, Inc., Publishers, 2011), 37–8, 40–1.

[2] Karen Hess, "Historical Notes and Commentaries on Mary Randolph's *The Virginia House-wife*," in *The Virginia House-wife by Mary Randolph: A Facsimile of the First Edition, 1824, Along with Additional Material from the Editions of 1825 and 1828, thus Presenting a Complete Text* (Columbia: University of South Carolina Press, 1984), 227.

The Story of Mary Randolph

[1] Haff, *Founders*, 38.

[2] Daniel Call, *Reports of Cases Argued and Adjudged in the Court of Appeals of Virginia* (Charlottesville, VA: The Michie Company, Law Publishers, 1902), 270.

[3] Duke de la Rochefoucauld-Liancourt, *Travels Through the United States of North America* 2nd ed. vol. 3 (London: T. Gillet, 1800), 112–13; and Jonathan Daniels, *The Randolphs of Virginia* (Garden City, NJ: Doubleday & Company, Inc., 1972), 131.

[4] Daniels, *Randolphs*, 196.

[5] Haff, *Founders*, 38; Longdone, "Introduction," 7; and Hess, "Historical Notes," xi, xl.

[6] Mary Randolph, *The Virginia Housewife* (New York: Dover Publications, Inc., 1993), iii-iv.

[7] La Rochefoucauld, *Travels*, 115.

[8] Samuel Mordecai, *Richmond in By-Gone Days* (Richmond, VA: George M. West, 1856), 97; and Haff, *Founders*, 39.

[9] Daniels, *Randolphs*, 197–99. Quotation, 199.

[10] Mordecai, *Richmond*, 97.

[11] Haff, *Founders*, 39; and Jane Carson, *Colonial Virginia Cookery* (Williamsburg, VA: The Colonial Williamsburg Foundation, 1985), xix–xx. Gabriel frequently appears as Gabriel Prosser, the surname coming from his owner Thomas Prosser.

[12] Daniels, *Randolphs*, 200.

[13] Ibid., 199–200.

[14] Harman Blennerhassett, *The Blennerhassett Papers* (Cincinnati, OH: Moore, Wilstach & Baldwin, 1864), 457–58.

[15] Ann T. Keene, "Randolph, Mary," *American National Biography*, eds. John A Garraty and Mark C. Carnes, 24 vols. (New York: Oxford University Press, 1999), 18:132; and Bennett Woodcroft, *Subject-Matter Index (Made From Titles Only), From March 2, 1617 (14 James I.), to October 1, 1852 (16 Victoriæ). Part I.—(A-M.)* London: Commissioners of Patents, 1857), 76, 188.

[16] Haff, *Founders*, 39.

[17] Kenne, "Randolph, Mary," 18:132; Daniels, *Randolphs*, 197, 202; and *The Papers of Thomas Jefferson, Retirement Series, vol. 9 1 September 1815 to 30 April 1816*, ed. J. Jefferson Looney (Princeton, NJ: Princeton University Press, 2012), 101n.

[18] *Papers of Thomas Jefferson*, 9:100.

[19] Ibid., 9:100.

[20] Mordecai, *Richmond*, 97.

[21] As quoted in Margaret Husted, "Mary Randloph's *The Virginia Housewife*: America's First Regional Cookbook," *Virginia Cavalcade* 30 no. 2 (Autumn 1980):80–1.

[22] As quoted in Harry Kollatz, Jr., *True Richmond Stories: Historic Tales from Virginia's Capital* (Mt. Pleasant, SC: The History Press, 2007), 43; and Haff, *Founders*, 39.

[23] Mordecai, *Richmond*, 97.

[24] Carson, *Colonial Virginia Cookery*, xix–xx.

[25] Mordecai, *Richmond*, 97.

[26] *A List of Patents Granted by the United States from April 10, 1790 to December 31, 1836* (Washington, DC: Commissioner of Patents, 1872), 154.

[27] Daniels, *Randolphs*, 247–8. For example, David patented an improved way to tap liquor barrels in 1821. *List of Patents*, 227.

Cookery Books and Culinary Traditions in *The Virginia Housewife*

[1] Gilly Lehmann, The British Housewife: Cookery Books, Cooking and Society in Eighteenth–Century Britain (Blackawton, Totnes, Devon, UK: Prospect Books, 2003), 61.

[2] Lehman, British Housewife, 61–66. Statistics, 65.

[3] As quoted in Carson, *Colonial Virginia Cookery*, xiii; Janice B. Longone and Daniel T. Longone, *American Cookbooks and Wine Books, 1797–1950* (Ann Arbor, MI: The Clements Library, 1984), 1; and Eric Quayle, *Old Cook Books: An Illustrated History* (New York: The Brandywine Press, Inc., 1978), 131.

[4] As quoted in Helen Bullock, *The Williamsburg Art of Cookery* (Williamsburg, VA: Colonial Williamsburg, 1972), vi.

[5] Carson, *Colonial Virginia Cookery*, xii–xiv; Longone and Longone, *American Cookbooks*, 1; and Quayle, *Old Cook Books*, 131–32.

[6] As quoted in Hess, "Historical Notes," xix.

[7] Hess, "Historical Notes," xix–xx; and Sandra L. Oliver, *Food in Colonial and Federal America* (Westport, CT: Greenwood Press, 2005), 1. Hess puts the recipe count at twenty-nine.

[8] Longone and Longone, *American Cookbooks*, 1–2; and Quayles, *Old Cook Books*, 138.

[9] Karen Hess, *Martha Washington's Booke of Cookery* (New York: Columbia University Press, 1981), 3, 7.

[10] Katharine E. Harbury, *Colonial Virginia's Cooking Dynasty* (Columbia: University of South Carolina Press, 2004), xiii–xvi.

[11] Randolph, *Virginia Housewife*, iv.

[12] Ibid., 176–80.

[13] Ibid., iv.

[14] Hess, "Historical Notes," viii–ix.

[15] Randolph, *Virginia Housewife*, iii.

[16] As quoted in Husted, "Mary Randolph's," 82.

[17] Hess, "Historical Notes," xxxiii.

[18] Lorena S. Walsh, "Consumer Behavior, Diet, and the Standard of Living in Late Colonial and Early Antebellum America, 1770–1840," paper presented to the Institute of Early American History and Culture, Williamsburg, VA, September 25, 1990, 11, John D. Rockefeller Jr. Library, Colonial Williamsburg Foundation, Williamsburg, VA.

[19] Husted, "Mary Randolph's," 84.

[20] Randolph, *Virginia Housewife*, 100–01.

[21] Ibid., 109.

[22] Ibid., 105.

[23] Ibid., 108.

[24] Walsh, "Consumer Behavior," 12.

[25] Hess, "Historical Notes," xxvi, xxxiii.

[26] Ibid., xxvi–xxxii, xxxviii.

[27] Hess and Hess, "Taste of America," 93.

Mary Randolph and Her Legacy

1 Randolph, *Virginia Housewife*, iii.

2 Haff, *Founders*, 42. For Beecher, see Catherine E. Beecher, *A Treatise on Domestic Economy: For the Use of Young Ladies at Home, and at School*, Revised Ed. (Boston: Thomas H. Webb, & Co., 1843) and Catherine E. Beecher and Harriet Beecher Stowe, *The American Woman's Home, or, Principles of Domestic Science: Being a Guide to the Formation and Maintenance of Economical, Healthful, Beautiful, and Christian Homes* (New York: J.B. Ford & CO., 1869).

3 Husted, "Mary Randolph's," 85.

4 Mary Randolph, *The Virginia House-Wife. Method is the Soul of Management* (Washington, DC: Printed by Davis and Force, 1824), xi; and Husted, "Mary Randolph's," 82. Some authors mistakenly have claimed that Randolph published the first edition anonymously. See Keene, "Randolph, Mary," 18:133 and Quayle, *Old Cook Books*, 138.

5 M. Randolph, *The Virginia House-Wife. Method is the Soul of Management. Second Edition, with Amendments and Additions* (Washington, DC: Printed by Way & Gideon, 1825), Inserts 1–3 between 256–57, 259–61; and *Carson*, "Colonial Virginia Cookery," xx.

6 Mary Randolph to James Madison, March 17, 1825, James Madison Papers, 1723 to 1859: Series 1, General Correspondence, 1723–1859, Library of Congress, Washington, DC, loc.gov/item/mjm019536.

7 James Madison to Mary Randolph, March 26, 1825, James Madison Papers, 1723 to 1859: Series 1, General Correspondence, 1723–1859, Library of Congress, Washington, DC, loc.gov/item/mjm019544.

8 Husted, "Mary Randolph's," 82

9 As quoted in Daniels, *Randolphs*, 248.

10 Letitia M. Burwell, *A Girl's Life in Virginia Before the War* (New York: Frederick A. Stokes Company Publishers, 1895), 39.

11 Susan Dabney Smedes, *Memorials of a Southern Planter* (Baltimore: Cushings & Bailey, 1887), 33.

12 Hess, "Historical Notes," ix.

13 Husted, "Mary Randloph's, 77.

14 Longone, "Introduction," 3–4.

BIBLIOGRAPHY

Primary Sources

Beecher, Catherine E. *A Treatise on Domestic Economy: For the Use of Young Ladies at Home, and at School.* Revised Ed. Boston: Thomas H. Webb, & Co., 1843.

_____ and Harriet Beecher Stowe. *The American Woman's Home, or, Principles of Domestic Science: Being a Guide to the Formation and Maintenance of Economical, Healthful, Beautiful, and Christian Homes.* New York: J.B. Ford & CO., 1869.

Blennerhassett, Harman. *The Blennerhassett Papers.* Cincinnati, OH: Moore, Wilstach & Baldwin, 1864.

Burwell, Letitia M. *A Girl's Life in Virginia Before the War.* New York: Frederick A. Stokes Company Publishers, 1895.

Call, Daniel. *Reports of Cases Argued and Adjudged in the Court of Appeals of Virginia.* Charlottesville, VA: The Michie Company, Law Publishers, 1902.

James Madison Papers, 1723 to 1859: Series 1, General Correspondence, 1723-1859. Library of Congress, Washington, DC.

Jefferson, Thomas. *The Papers of Thomas Jefferson, Retirement Series*, vol. 9 *1 September 1815 to 30 April 1816.* Edited by J. Jefferson Looney. Princeton, NJ: Princeton University Press, 2012.

La Rochefoucauld-Liancourt, Duke de. *Travels Through the United States of North America.* 2nd ed. Vol. 3 London: T. Gillet, 1800.

A List of Patents Granted by the United States from April 10, 1790 to December 31, 1836. Washington, DC: Commissioner of Patents, 1872.

Madison, James. Letter to Mary Randolph, March 26, 1825. James Madison Papers, 1723 to 1859: Series 1, General Correspondence, 1723-1859. Library of Congress, Washington, DC. http://www.loc.gov/item/mjm019544 .

Mordecai, Samuel. *Richmond in By-Gone Days.* Richmond, VA: George M. West, 1856.

Randolph, Mary. Letter to James Madison, March 17, 1825. James Madison Papers, 1723 to 1859: Series 1, General Correspondence, 1723-1859. Library of Congress, Washington, DC. https://www.loc.gov/item/mjm019536/ .

_____. *The Virginia House-Wife by Mary Randolph: A Facsimile of the First Edition, 1824, Along with Additional Material from the Editions of 1825 and 1828, thus Presenting a Complete Text.* Edited by Karen Hess. Columbia: University of South Carolina Press, 1984.

_____. *The Virginia House-Wife. Method is the Soul of Management.* Washington, DC: Printed by Davis and Force, 1824.

_____. *The Virginia House-Wife. Method is the Soul of Management. Second Edition, with Amendments and Additions.* Washington, DC: Printed by Way and Gideon, 1825.

_____. *The Virginia Housewife: Or Methodical Cook.* Philadelphia: E.H. Butler & Co., 1860.

_____. *The Virginia Housewife, or, Methodical Cook: A Facsimile of an Authentic Early American Cookbook.* New York: Dover Publications, Inc., 1993.

Smedes, Susan Dabney. *Memorials of a Southern Planter* (Baltimore: Cushings & Bailey, 1887.

Woodcroft, Bennett. *Subject-Matter Index (Made From Titles Only), From March 2, 1617 (14 James I.), to October 1, 1852 (16 Victoriæ). Part I.—(A-M.)* London: Commissioners of Patents, 1857.

Secondary Materials

Bullock, Helen. *The Williamsburg Art of Cookery.* Williamsburg, VA: Colonial Williamsburg, 1972.

Carson, Jane. *Colonial Virginia Cookery.* Williamsburg, VA: The Colonial Williamsburg Foundation, 1985.

Daniels, Jonathan. *The Randolphs of Virginia.* Garden City, NJ: Doubleday & Company, Inc., 1972.

Haff, Harry. *The Founders of American Cuisine.* Jefferson, NC: McFarland & Company, Inc., Publishers, 2011.

Harbury, Katharine E. *Colonial Virginia's Cooking Dynasty.* Columbia: University of South Carolina Press, 2004.

Hess, John L. and Karen Hess. *The Taste of America.* Columbia: University of South Carolina Press, 1989.

Hess, Karen. *Martha Washington's Booke of Cookery.* New York: Columbia University Press, 1981.

_____. "Historical Notes and Commentaries on Mary Randolph's *The Virginia House-Wife*." In *The Virginia House-wife by Mary Randolph: A Facsimile of the First Edition, 1824, Along with Additional Material from the Editions of 1825 and 1828, thus Presenting a Complete Text.* Columbia: University of South Carolina Press, 1984: ix-xlv.

Husted, Margaret. "Mary Randolph's *The Virginia Housewife*: America's First Regional Cookbook." *Virginia Cavalcade* 30 no. 2 (Autumn 1980): 76-87.

Keene, Ann T. "Randolph, Mary." *American National Biography*, eds. John A Garraty and Mark C. Carnes, 24 vols. New York: Oxford University Press, 1999, 18:132-133.

Lehmann, Gilly. *The British Housewife: Cookery Books, Cooking and Society in Eighteenth-Century Britain.* Blackawton, Totnes, Devon, UK: Prospect Books, 2003.

Longone, Janice Bluestein. "Introduction to the Dover Edition." In *The Virginia Housewife or, Methodical Cook: A Facsimile of an Authentic Early American Cookbook.* New York: Dover Publications, Inc., 1993: 3-7.

_____ and Daniel T. Longone. *American Cookbooks and Wine Books, 1797-1950.* Ann Arbor, MI: The Clements Library, 1984.

Oliver, Sandra L. *Food in Colonial and Federal America.* Westport, CT: Greenwood Press, 2005.

Quayle, Eric. *Old Cook Books: An Illustrated History.* New York: The Brandywine Press, Inc., 1978.

Walsh, Lorena S. "Consumer Behavior, Diet, and the Standard of Living in Late Colonial and Early Antebellum America, 1770-1840." Paper presented to the Institute of Early American History and Culture, Williamsburg, VA, September 25, 1990. John D. Rockefeller Jr. Library, Colonial Williamsburg Foundation, Williamsburg, VA.

INDEX

ABOUT THE AUTHORS

Brian J. Martine

Sue J. Hendricks is a native of Martinsville, Virginia, and life-long cook. She is a former writer and editor for the *Winston-Salem Journal*, where she developed the monthly periodical, *K-12*. She is the author of *100 Years of Images: Capturing the Moment*. Her son **Christopher E. Hendricks** is Professor of History at the Armstrong Campus of Georgia Southern University in Savannah, where he has taught since 1993. He is the author of numerous publications, including *The Backcountry Towns of Colonial Virginia*.